JOSHUA:
A MAN OF THE FINGER LAKES REGION

A TRUE STORY TAKEN FROM LIFE

BY

CHARLES BRUTCHER

E P B M

ECHO POINT BOOKS & MEDIA, LLC

Published in 2017 by Echo Point Books & Media
Brattleboro, Vermont
www.EchoPointBooks.com

Preface copyright © 2017 by Echo Point Books & Media

Joshua: A Man of the Finger Lakes Region
ISBN: 978-1-62654-157-3 (casebound)
          978-1-63561-730-6 (paperback)

Cover image and typography by Justine McFarland
Cover design by Justine McFarland

DEDICATION

To Melvin J. Rosekrans, who has assisted
in the preparation of this work

Joshua Rosecamp, "A Man of the Finger Lakes Region"

CONTENTS

vi   CONTENTS

LIST OF ILLUSTRATIONS

PREFACE

After adjusting for inflation, John D. Rockefeller is the richest human to have ever lived. That feat alone is worthy of inquiry. But more significant is the outsized influence he has had on modern industrial capitalism. More than anyone else, he perfected the art and artifice of the modern corporate conglomerate and used it for massive political and economic influence. There are good reasons anti-trust legislation focused on Standard Oil.

But Rockefeller's notable influence didn't stop with the economy; he also had a significant impact on politics and philanthropy. By learning about Rockefeller the man, one gains insight into who we are as Americans and how we have arrived at our current state of affairs economically, politically, and culturally. And if you wish to truly understand the man and his influences, you would do well to understand his father.

John D. Rockefeller was a complex fellow. He was a moralist who could expound upon and follow strict ethics in the morning, and then in the afternoon crush a perceived business opponent— as a mafia Don might squash a rival (except instead of guns and brass knuckles, his weapons were financial cost cutting, backroom deals, and political influence that bent business regulations in his favor). When it came to business, his love of money would hijack his moral compass, often wrapped in high-hatted rationalizations. These justifications allowed him to treat his ruthless pursuit of business interests as a virtuous crusade.

Where did that love of money and need for righteousness and respectability come from? It's hard not to see his father's influence. William "Big Bill" Rockefeller was a bigamist and flim-flam hustler who peddled secret potions and elixirs hundreds of miles from home. When he was far away on the road plying his phony wares, hunger and poverty were near for the family he left behind. John D. Rockefeller's mother often had a large overdue tab at the local grocery store and was forced to beg and cajole the owner for her next order. She was kept upright and strong by her deep religious faith.

Not a lot is known of John D. Rockefeller's father, but one of the few detailed sources comes from this book by Charles Brutcher, *Joshua: A Man of Finger Lakes Region*. Here is what Ron Chernow wrote about *Joshua: A Man of Finger Lakes Region* in Titan, his brilliant, prize-winning biography about John D. Rockefeller:

> Given the paucity of hard evidence about [Rockefeller's] affairs in Moravia, one is left to rake over the rich folklore he left behind. In 1927, a carpenter turned author named Charles Brutcher published a book entitled *Joshua: A Man of the Finger Lakes Region*, a thinly disguised roman à clef about William Avery Rockefeller. The privately printed 130-page book has become something of a collector's item, with copies sometimes fetching hundreds of dollars. The protagonist is one William Rockwell, a.k.a Big Bill, and the author brazenly mingles fact and fiction by reproducing an actual photo of Rockefeller's father in the front. Joshua professes, redundantly, to be a "true story taken from life" and gathers lore about Devil Bill that was still titillating the town gossips in the 1920s. Much of its store of legend came from Melvin Rosekrans, whose father, Joshua, had locked horns with Big Bill in the 1840s. The book presents a slanted, hyperbolic portrait of Big Bill's career, a compendium of his presumed misdeeds, yet enough details tally with documentary material from other sources that it merits review.

As Chernow points out, little is known about Big Bill. *Joshua* is the closest we can come to direct insight into his life and personality. I believe you'll find him an interesting character in his own right. Enjoy.

—Fred Murdie, Echo Point Books & Media

INTRODUCTION

THIS story is taken from life, all the characters in this book really existed and enacted the scenes brought before the eyes of the reader.

The book deals with the lives and history of the early settlers of the Finger Lakes region and some very strange incidents are disclosed, so strange in fact that one wonders at the almost incredulous tales of adventure that happened right in the heart of our Empire State.

Owasco Lake, the most picturesque of the Finger Lakes, lies near the city of Auburn, extending from there to the quaint old village of Moravia, which is located near its further, or southern end. Around this lake many of the scenes of this entrancing narrative are laid.

At the time of our story the peaceful countryside was terrorized by a band of desperadoes and horse thieves, whose operations extended over several counties.

A sigh of relief went up from the long suffering old settlers when the gang was finally broken up, and its notorious leader, William Rockwell, driven out of the state.

One experiences a queer sensation when finding one's self, as the author has, in the identical places where the stirring incidents described in this book have taken place years ago.

For instance, at Rockwell's cave where the gang used to meet to plan their secret expeditions, or at the almost inaccessible gully which could only be reached by a hidden path and where the gang would assemble and hide the stolen horses.

It will be shown that this band operated in conjunction with the notorious Loomis gang from Oneida County.

Their history will also be found in this book.

Among the principal characters in this story, William Rockwell stands forth as the boldest, keenest and shrewdest of them all.

He organized a gang, unequalled in daring, whose members would stop at nothing, and who remained faithful and true to their leader to the very end.

William Rockwell was the father of John, who was destined to become one of the world's most powerful business men. John, a forceful character like his father, also developed a master mind, deriving from his father the peculiar faculty of organizing others to serve his own interests.

Joshua Rosecamp, son of John Rosecamp, a neighbor of William Rockwell, plays a leading role in this story.

Joshua incurred the enmity of Rockwell early in his career, when he became suspicious and started to watch his movements, eventually becoming his nemesis.

Rockwell in return persecuted Joshua, causing his arrest on a trumped-up charge, only to find himself caught in the meshes of the law.

Joshua's untiring efforts proved the means of Rockwell's ultimate downfall.

He was instrumental in bringing about his exposure and final banishment, reminding the reader that, "Right will triumph over might in the end."

Luella Green, Joshua's sweetheart and faithful companion, also takes a prominent part in this unusual story.

Luella, being employed by Rockwell, was in a position to keep Joshua informed in regard to the former's movements, proving herself a competent and trustworthy ally.

It was Luella who stood loyally by Joshua, bravely assisting him in the final exposure of the terror of the Finger Lakes region.

Dr. William Cooper, cousin of the famous Fenimore Cooper, author of "Leatherstocking Tales," enters into the story, first in his professional capacity, later through his valuable co-operation in breaking up the notorious gang.

Cale Parmer, never-do-well, Rockwell's lieutenant and faith-

ful accomplice, participated in all of Rockwell's unlawful
actions and was sent to prison in the end.

Brow Scott, nondescript brother-in-law of Joshua, allied himself with Rockwell early in his career, becoming one of his most
subservient tools. He also wound up in prison.

This story was inspired by Joshua Rosecamp, who lived in it
by day and dreamed of it at night.

He related the story of his eventful life to his son, Melvin, to
be confirmed later by a number of old settlers from Cayuga
County.

Melvin Rosecamp was instrumental in compiling this book.
He learned the story in its minutest detail from his father, who
was anxious to see it in book form.

Joshua's dream was never realized.

Owing to Melvin's energy and persistency the book was
eventually written and it is now before the public.

The book will prove interesting reading and the reader will
be reminded more than once of the old adage: "Truth is even
stranger than fiction."

THE AUTHOR

Joshua: A Man of the Finger Lakes Region

CHAPTER I

JOSHUA MAKES A DISCOVERY

JOSHUA ROSECAMP was looking out through the window of their farmhouse, one fine spring morning, when something unusual caught his attention. He rubbed his eyes and looked again to reassure himself, as he saw smoke curling from the chimney of the farmhouse next to their own. As far as he knew, the house had been vacant all winter, the owner, Lathrop Hewett having moved out late in the fall and the place had been vacant and for sale ever since.

"Well," said Joshua, more to himself, but loud enough for his father, who was in the room with him, to hear: "That certainly was quick work; someone must have moved in there in a hurry, like a thief in the night."

Joshua, or Josh as he was commonly called, was a young man about twenty years old at the time, of medium height, well built, strong and active, in short, he was a typical farmer lad.

"What's wrong, Josh?" asked his father who had noticed the strange behavior of his son, "are you seeing things?"

"Come and see for yourself, dad, and tell me what you think of it," and as his father joined him by the window, Josh pointed to the still smoking chimney.

"That's funny, I met Hewett only two weeks ago and he didn't say anything to me then about his farm being sold. Do you suppose some tramp broke in there to get a night's lodging?" replied his father.

"Well, that's possible, but I hardly think so; I'll go down to find out and I'll soon let you know," said Josh as he left the house.

John Rosecamp, Joshua's father, had lived on the old home-

stead all his life, in fact he had been born there. He had inherited the farm from his father who had been one of the earliest
pioneers and settlers in that part of the country.

Their farm was a few miles from the village of Moravia and
about a mile east of Owasco Lake, one of the finest lakes in
the state.

John's wife was dead, his daughter Ellen keeping house for
him and Joshua.

Ellen was married and had two children, but she and her
husband did not get on very well together. He very seldom
stayed at home. She had married one Brow Scott against the
wishes of her father and to her sorrow. Josh had taken a keen
dislike toward his brother-in-law, but he was very much attached to his sister Ellen.

Brow Scott, a shiftless character, who never worked steady
at anything and who was always mixed up in some shady trans-
action or other, barely managed to keep out of jail, hovering
near the prison gates like a moth around the flame.

Of him there will be more said later.

CHAPTER II

A STRANGE NEIGHBOR

IN the meantime Josh had started out on his quest and was walking down the road which led from their place to the main highway and right past the newly tenanted farmhouse.

It was a beautiful morning and Josh felt in high spirits as he approached the house, owned and. formerly occupied by Lathrop Hewett.

Just as he was about to enter, a powerfully built man of middle age stepped out of the rear door and perceiving Josh, hailed him with these words. "Hello, young feller, where are you bound for so early in the morning?"

"Oh, I happened to notice signs of life on this place and I wondered who was staying here. You know this house has been empty all winter. We didn't see anybody moving in, so I thought I'd find out about it," answered Josh.

"Oh, that's it," said the stranger, laughing good naturedly. "I did move in kind of sudden; we didn't get here till late last night; the trip took longer than I figured. You know it's quite a ways from Richport, Tioga County; that's where I came from.

"My name is Bill Rockwell; everybody calls me 'Big Bill,' though. I just bought this place last week. Do you live around here?"

"Yes, that's our place up there," replied Josh, pointing to his father's house, about half a mile away from where they stood.

"We're your nearest neighbors."

The Rosecamp farm lay higher than Hewett's place, both of them being located on a hillside, gently sloping toward Lake Owasco.

"My name is Josh Rosecamp," and Josh held out his hand which the other shook in a friendly fashion, inviting him at the same time to step inside.

3

"No, some other time'll do," answered Josh.

"I got to get back to do the chores, but we're right glad to have a neighbor once more. It's been kind of lonesome since old Hewett moved out. Say, if we can do anything for you let us know and we'll be glad to help you out."

"Thanks," replied Rockwell, "that's good of you, I might call on you sooner than you expect."

"Oh, that's all right, you're welcome any time," said Josh, as he went on his way.

"Oh, say," Rockwell called after him, "you and your folks come and see us some time."

CHAPTER III

The Terror of the Finger Lakes Region

WELL they might call him "Big Bill," for he was a splendid specimen of manhood, well over six feet tall and built in proportion. He carried himself like an athlete and he certainly didn't look the part of a farmer, rather that of a country gentleman. Truly a commanding figure, with strength and will power written all over him. A kindly face with ever a smile, a pair of keen blue eyes which seemed to appraise one at a glance, a sport and good fellow to all appearances and a born leader of men. He wore a full beard, which gave him the appearance of a statesman of that period.

Rockwell had been in this part of the country before, when, some years previously, he had married the daughter of a prosperous farmer by the name of Davis, much against the wishes of her family. The affair had been pulled off so quietly during one of "Big Bill's" mysterious trips that not even the immediate neighbors had been aware of it until after Eliza Davis had left with Rockwell for Richport, her new home.

Otherwise little was known of "Big Bill" by the people of Moravia, because he never tarried long in any one place. He was a man of mystery to all of them.

His father, Godfrey Rockwell, had brought his family from Massachusetts to Richport, where they lived for a few years.

Godfrey Rockwell was a man who had failed to make his mark in life; one of those unfortunate beings who simply exist for a time and die; a shiftless tippler with no aim in life.

His wife, on the other hand, was a remarkable woman in many ways, highly intelligent and determined in all of her actions, and it is from his mother, no doubt, that William Rockwell inherited his dominating personality.

He learned his lesson early in life; his father's loose and in-

5

William Rockwell or "Big Bill"

dulgent habits made a lasting impression on young William, for he never drank.

When he first came to Tioga County with his parents and later when he would be gone on his periodical peddling trips, he played up deaf and dumb, until he was exposed. In this way he undoubtedly gathered information which later on became of great assistance to him in executing his daring deeds.

Such is the man that injected himself into this peaceful community of old settlers, who lived a quiet life among themselves, unsuspecting of the wolf in sheep's clothes who had dared to appear in their midst; the man who was to startle and shock the inhabitants of Moravia and surrounding towns and become the terror of the Finger Lakes region.

Little did Josh dream what the arrival of this stranger would mean to him, to his family and to his neighbors and what a disturbing element had entered into their well regulated and simple lives.

William Rockwell's evil influence would be felt in every household for miles around.

Joshua Rosecamp's Boyhood Home

CHAPTER IV

A Friendly Call

AFTER Josh returned. home from his visit to their new neighbor, his father naturally asked him what he had found out.

"You can't guess, dad. Why, we got a new neighbor, and believe me he is some neighbor."

Josh then went on to describe him, told his name and all he had learned about him.

"Oh, I guess I know him," his father remarked, after Josh had furnished him with a minute description of Rockwell.

"If it's the man I have in mind, he is quite a talker and a jolly good feller. He used to travel through this part of the country off and on in years gone by, but he never impressed me as being much of a farmer. He looks more like a country doctor, and come to think of it, he is some kind of a quack at that."

"That's the man all right," agreed Josh.

This section of the country consisted largely of good, rich farm land and was noted for agriculture.

The old settlers also raised some fine horses which found their way to surrounding towns and cities, even as far as the metropolis, where they always found a ready market.

A large part of the countryside was covered with woods. The farmers would cut out the logs, draw them down to Owasco Lake, where they would be formed into rafts and floated on the lake to Prison City, to be sawed into lumber.

John Rosecamp was a breeder of good horses, noted for it and well known all over. He and his son, Josh, raised and sold horses, receiving the highest prices for them, besides working their farm.

9

A few days after the arrival of their new neighbor, Josh and his father called on Rockwell and were met with a hearty welcome.

"Well, neighbor," said old John, as they entered the newcomer's house and shook hands, "we thought we'd call on you and bid you welcome to our town, but it strikes me that we have met before."

"Most likely we have," answered Rockwell with a laugh. "I've traveled around quite a bit in my days and I've been in this part of the country before. You know my wife is a Davis girl; her folks own a farm a few miles from here."

"Why, yes, now I remember you, you used to sell horses them days," said old John.

"I do yet," replied "Big Bill." "I buy and sell horses. Any time you know of some good ones, let me know and I'll make it worth your while. There is more money in handling horses than there is in farming."

"Well, yes, we are raising horses too. We got some purty fair ones on hand right now, but we got our regular customers for them. You must come up and see them." Old John then changed the subject and inquired about Rockwell's family, whereupon "Big Bill" introduced his wife, a sad faced little woman, who greeted father and son with a smile.

John, the oldest boy, who was about eight years old at the time, was a sickly looking lad with keen, piercing eyes like his father's and he was scrutinizing the two strangers closely.

Besides him there were two smaller boys, Frank and William.

"Do you calculate to work your farm alone or do you intend to hire some help?" queeried old John.

"Yes and no. It depends on what help I can get around here. Anyway, I don't figure on doing much farming, and besides I am away from home a good deal," said "Big Bill."

After a few more commonplace remarks his neighbors left, bidding him good-bye.

CHAPTER V

ROCKWELL'S FRIENDS

AFTER Rockwell got accustomed to his new surroundings, it began to be noticed that he had gathered certain men around him to assist him in his work—men who were considered worthless characters, and who were shunned by their neighbors.

There was one Cale Parmer, in particular, who lived about a mile from "Big Bill's" place.

He would hardly be out of one scrape before he would become involved in another. None of his neighbors associated with him.

He was not considered a good and reliable citizen. He would work only when the notion overtook him and his farm was very much run down.

Cale lived with his wife and three boys in a big rambling house on the highest point of a plateau overlooking the countryside for miles around.

From his house a splendid view could be had of Owasco Lake, one of the prettiest lakes in the state. Possessing a wonderful shore line, blended with beautiful scenery, the lake lies in a deep depression, surrounded by plateaus rising to a considerable height.

Queer and ugly stories were being told about Cale.

Warren Austen, one of his neighbors, had some words with Cale over some of his cows that had strayed on Austen's land, doing considerable damage there.

One morning, following his altercation with Cale, Austen found his orchard of fifty young fruit trees cut down. All the trees had been cut from the left hand side and it was plain to be seen that the dastardly deed had been committed by a left handed person.

11

Cale Parmer was the only left handed man known thereabouts.

After a thorough investigation, the act of vandalism was traced to Cale; the footprints in the soft earth corresponding exactly with Cale's.

He was arrested and held for the grand jury, which soon found an indictment against him. Following his trial and conviction he served some time in Prison City and was released just before the beginning of our story.

This was only one of many occasions where Cale had come in conflict with the law.

It was common talk among the neighbors and generally accepted as truth that strangers, who had stayed over night at Cale's house, had been robbed of their valuables and money.

There was one other, Brow Scott, who made Rockwell's place his temporary home. He and Cale Parmer had been associates, even before Rockwell's coming.

Brow Scott, of ill-repute, who was accused of being a counterfeiter and forger and although he had never been convicted, spurious money and worthless paper had been traced back to him on different occasions.

Scott had formerly lived near Richport in Tioga County, where be became acquainted with Rockwell.

He used to accompany the latter on his periodical trips and it was on one of these that he got stranded at Moravia and became acquainted with Ellen Rosecamp whom he married, after a short courtship. Ellen had discovered her husband's wayward and shiftless disposition soon after their marriage and she was strongly opposed to it. She had tried her best, time and again, to induce Scott to change his mode of living, but without success.

Rockwell's evil influence and dominating power had won out over her wifely devotion. Scott had chosen to follow "Big Bill's" lead.

Some call it magnetism, but it is simply mind over matter, a strong mind imposing its will over a weaker one.

Ellen, Brow Scott's Wife

While Scott remained at home with his wife and children and even after he made Rockwell's place his temporary abode, he imparted valuable information concerning Rockwell's doings to his wife, Ellen. These disclosures became, as we will show later, of great assistance to her brother Josh, in whom she confided.

Both Parmer and Scott were hanging around "Big Bill's" place and they could be seen doing odd jobs there at most any time.

Rockwell's nearest neighbor, besides Rosecamp, was Jim Hewett.

A deep ravine, known as Hewett's gully, separated their two farms. Of this gully there will be some interesting developments in the following chapter.

The gully proved a bone of contention between Rockwell and Jim Hewett, each one claiming it, after the former bought Lathrop Hewett's farm. They had some litigation over the possession of the gully, but in the end they declared a truce and it was left an open question between the two. Whatever their real feelings were, outwardly they remained friendly toward each other.

The neighbors insinuated that their fight over the gully was merely a blind to keep inquisitive visitors away from there. Succeeding events will tend to strengthen their contention.

The townspeople called it Hewett's gully. It was really a deep ravine which ended at Owasco Lake, about two miles from its starting point. An awe-inspiring sight greets the eye and sends shivers down one's spine when peering into the deep chasm from the overhanging bridge.

The ravine is dry except in the spring and fall when the waters from the surrounding plateaus find their way down in there and transform it into a raging torrent.

No better hiding place for man or beast could be found.

CHAPTER VI

JOSHUA'S FIRST ADVENTURE

SOME two months after Rockwell's arrival in Moravia, Josh was on his way home from a visit to the Green family, who lived near the village, and it was quite late. He had to cross Hewett's gully and as he was walking over the old wooden bridge, spanning the gully at a height of nearly one hundred feet, he detected a faint glimmer of light coming from a point in the gully quite a distance farther up from the bridge.

He stopped dead in his tracks and listened, but no sound came to him. At first he thought someone had wandered or fallen down there accidentally and that a searching party was down below.

The gully was dry at this time of the year, it being summer, but it could only be reached by a path leading down to it about half a mile from the bridge.

He saw the light moving as if someone was carrying it and he decided to investigate. He left the highway and scrambled slowly up through the wooded slope, skirting the gully on both sides. As he came nearer to the flickering light he heard voices and his wonder increased.

Josh knew no fear, he had been taught early in life to be self-dependent and he was well able to take care of himself. Instinct told him that something unusual was taking place right under his very eyes and he became more cautious, so as not to make himself known.

After venturing as close as he dared, he peered through the bushes. The gully widened out at this point, becoming more shallow and forming a sort of basin. The path leading into it from the upper end was only a short distance from where he stood. As his eyes got accustomed to the semi-darkness, he

15

made out some dim shapes, and there came to his ears the muffled sound of voices and the stamping of horses.

Suddenly it flashed across his mind—horse thieves!

He remained perfectly quiet and watched the scene before him, tense and alert.

If he could only tell who the men were.

The light from a single lantern was too poor to distinguish their faces.

Two of the figures appeared strangely familiar to him; one in particular, the big, powerfully built man reminded him instantly of Rockwell, their new neighbor.

Fascinated and not daring to move for fear of betraying himself, he watched the big man as he examined the horses one by one, making entries in a small book by the light of the lantern.

Josh stayed where he was until the men leading the horses, which had been tied together, made their way in single file out through the upper end of the gully and disappeared in the darkness.

In all, Josh had counted four men and twelve horses. He was in a quandary and the whole proceeding seemed like a nightmare to him, reminding him of some wild western tales he had read. The thought of a band of horse thieves operating right in their midst had never entered his mind.

He was torn between conflicting emotions to go home and arouse his father, or to go and notify the sheriff, whom he could not reach in much less than an hour. By that time the mysterious strangers and their horses would be miles away.

Josh finally decided to go home first to get his father's opinion about the unheard of proceeding he had just witnessed.

He knew his father possessed good sound judgment and he trusted him implicitly. Hurrying home as fast as he could travel, he entered the barn first to see if their horses were all there; to his great relief he found them all safe. Instead of waking his father who was asleep when he got home, Josh went to his own room and retired. It would be time enough to tell his father in the morning.

Old John Rosecamp was a man of very few words, deliberate in his speech and slow to render an opinion, in fact he was a better listener than a talker. So, when his son related his unusual experience from the night before, he cautioned him to keep quiet until they would learn more about the mysterious affair.

"It looks mighty queer, Josh," he finally ventured, after a long silence, "are you sure that Rockwell was one of the men you saw there?"

After Josh had assured him that their new neighbor had been the principal actor in the scene he had witnessed, the old man went on and said: "It looks to me as if the horses had been stolen in some other part of the country and driven here by the men you didn't recognize, else they would have delivered them to Rockwell's place and in the daytime.

"So that's their hiding place, the old ravine. Well, they couldn't find a better one."

Josh went down to "Big Bill's" place early that same morning to see if he was home. Mrs. Rockwell informed him that her husband and Brow Scott had gone away together to look at some horses Bill intended to buy. She couldn't tell when they would be back.

Josh knew then that he was on the right track and his worst fears were confirmed.

He visited the gully that same day and found the imprints of horses' hoofs in the soft ground; mute evidence of the happenings of the night before.

Brow Scott was back inside of a week but Rockwell did not return until two weeks later and when he did, he had no horses with him.

In the meantime father and son were anxiously waiting to hear reports about missing horses. When no complaints were forthcoming, they concluded that the horses Josh had seen on that eventful night, had been delivered from distant parts.

After "Big Bill's" return, Josh made frequent trips to Hewett's gully at all hours of the night, expecting to witness another rendezvous, but nothing more took place there to further arouse his suspicions.

Mrs. Rockwell was not a very strong woman physically, and to perform her household duties for a family of five, besides the two roustabouts, Cale Parmer and Brow Scott, proved too much of a task for her. So "Big Bill" engaged the services of Luella Green to assist his wife with the housework. Luella's parents, who were in poor circumstances, lived on a small farm near the village of Moravia. At first they were opposed to have their daughter work for strangers, but they yielded to her earnest entreaties to contribute her share to their support and allowed her to work out.

Luella, or Lu as she was known to her friends, was a good looking and exceptionally bright young miss of eighteen summers.

Josh had known Lu since their childhood days. They had gone to the same school together and a warm friendship had sprung up between the two. Their friendship had ripened into love in later years, and while Josh had not yet declared himself, they understood each other thoroughly, more than mere words could express.

Lu used to come over to spend an evening with the Rosecamp family whenever it was possible for her to do so. She was always a welcome visitor at their house.

Ellen, sister of Josh, had taken a great liking to Lu, displaying a motherly interest in her brother's sweetheart.

CHAPTER VII

JACK FEEK

ABOUT this time John Rosecamp adopted a poor orphan by the name of Jack Feek.

John was getting along in years and it was his desire that Josh should have a companion to assist him in the care of their horses. Jack was a strong, willing boy, quite intelligent and quick to learn, adapting himself easily to his new surroundings.

He and Josh became great friends and boon companions. Jack being an apt pupil, he was fast acquiring all knowledge pertaining to horses under the instructions of Josh, who understood horses thoroughly and who was willing to impart to his young friend all he knew in that line.

In later years Jack Feek entered the services of a millionaire in Salt City, who was a great horse fancier. His horses were kept in a palatial stable and he spared no expense where horses were concerned. Jack remained with his employer until the latter's death when he was handsomely remembered in his will.

CHAPTER VIII

ROCKWELL'S FAMILY

CALE PARMER had been working steady for "Big Bill" for some time now. He stayed at his house while "Big Bill" was away on his trip after leaving the gully with his train of horses on the night Josh experienced the surprise of his life.

Cale knew his employer's destination, being in his confidence, but he kept it strictly to himself.

Between Rockwell, Brow Scott and himself, they worked "Big Bill's" farm in a haphazard way, in order to keep up the pretense of being industrious farmers, before the neighbors.

Mrs. Rockwell was kept in ignorance of the real motives underlying her husband's mysterious and irregular trips away from home. To her credit be it said, that she never would become a party to his shady transactions, even had she been aware of the fact. On the contrary, she was always opposed to "Big Bill's" roving disposition and his evil minded tendencies.

If she suspected any wrong doing, she kept it strictly to herself, for the sake of their children.

Mrs. Rockwell took a deep interest in her three boys, while her wayward husband concerned himself very little about them, with the exception of John, the oldest, whom he idolized.

While John, the oldest boy resembled his mother more in appearance, he took after his father in more ways than one.

Frank and William, the other two boys, bore the image of their father, yet they possessed none of his wild and unruly ways. They were dull, uninteresting boys.

Even in those days John, the oldest, displayed an unsatiable greed for money. He was always scheming and devising ways and means to make money with the least exertion on his own part.

21

John attended the little country school nearby, where he was rated as one of the brightest scholars. He never associated with the other boys of his age and persistently kept his own counsel.

His father's influence dominated him completely and while he received his early training from his mother, he followed his father's advice in business matters. As John grew older he developed the same traits as his father, as far as cunning and shrewdness were concerned. No one ever bested him in a business deal.

Bridge over Gully where Rockwell Would Assemble the Stolen Horses

CHAPTER IX

The House of Mystery

ON the afternoon following Rockwell's hasty exit from Hewitt's gully with his three companions and their string of horses, a stranger came to "Big Bill's" house inquiring for him.

Mrs. Rockwell informed him that Bill had gone away for a few days and she couldn't tell when he would be back.

The stranger, who introduced himself as Corning, asked permission to put his horse in the barn as he intended to stay in the neighborhood for a short time.

Mrs. Rockwell referred him to Cale Parmer, who took care of his horse and showed him around the place.

Corning showed particular interest in "Big Bill's" horses, asking numerous questions about them, becoming quite inquisitive, which was not at all to Cale's liking. The stranger examined some of the horses rather closely, Cale thought.

Corning, reading distrust in the other's eyes, and in order to allay his suspicions, remarked casually: "I used to know your boss in Richport; that's where I'm from. I came here to see if I could buy a mate to the horse I'm driving. I know 'Big Bill' used to deal in horses when he lived down there. Did he buy any lately?"

"No," answered Cale. "You got here at the wrong time. He jest left last night to look over some horses he intends buying. It's hard telling when he'll be back, though."

"Yes, that's Bill all over, he used to be away from home a good deal when he lived in Richport," was Corning's comment.

"Oh say," it came to him as an afterthought, "is there any other farm around here, where they raise and sell horses?"

"Why, you might try Rosecamp's, on the farm next to ours," said Cale, pointing that way.

23

Corning went there, finding Josh and his father working in the field. After he stated the purpose of his visit, old John informed him that their horses were practically all sold, as they had orders booked for them from a dealer in the metropolis.

Both father and son were friendly and willing to talk to Corning until he made inquiries about Rockwell, their new neighbor.

"Oh, him; why he is the strangest neighbor we ever had," was old John's only comment.

After a few more remarks, Corning left and returning to Rockwell's place, he hunted up Cale, who asked him how he had made out.

"Guess I'm out of luck. They're nice people all right, but I couldn't make no dicker with them; the only thing for me to do is to go back the way I came. It's most too late to start out now. You don't happen to know of a place around here where I could stay over night, do you?"

"Well," answered Cale after some hesitation, "you can come up to my house if you ain't too particular."

Corning accepted the invitation readily, waiting for Cale to finish his chores, when they both started out for Cale's home.

Mrs. Parmer, a strapping woman of middle age was coming from the barn, carrying a pail of milk, just as they reached the house.

As Cale introduced him to his wife, Corning caught a look passing between them which puzzled him for the moment, a look of reproach on the woman's part, reassuring on the man's.

They entered the house together and Mrs. Parmer, who appeared to be a hard working woman, prepared supper for them.

Afterward the two men smoked and talked. Parmer produced some home made wine, of which both men partook freely in the course of the evening.

Corning tried in every way to draw Cale out regarding Rockwell and his affairs, but Cale was on his guard, and would not divulge anything concerning his employer.

"He sure is a queer one. I always wondered why he left Rich-port in such a hurry," offered Corning after awhile, but Cale showed no inclination to prolong the conversation along those lines. He remained non-committal throughout the whole evening whenever "Big Bill's" name was mentioned.

Only once did Cale betray any interest, when the stranger spoke up and said:

"Does 'Big Bill' sell any more of his medicine when he travels through the country?"

"I couldn't say as to that. All I know is that he always carries a satchel with him when he goes on a trip. Shouldn't wonder if he does, 'cause he's flush with money whenever he gets back home."

Their conversation was carried on in the same vein for awhile longer until Corning became drowsy and expressed his desire to go to bed. Cale showed him to his room on the second floor where he had a number of spare rooms, the Parmer house being more like a country hotel than a farmhouse.

When Corning came down stairs the next morning he found Mrs. Parmer in the kitchen and upon inquiring for her husband, she informed him that he had gone down to Rockwell's to do the chores. She invited him to stay and have some breakfast.

After eating, the stranger asked Mrs. Parmer how much he owed them.

"Why, you owe us nothing; we wouldn't think of taking any money for a night's lodging and a few vittels," Mrs. Parmer assured him.

Intending to repay his hosts for their hospitality, Corning reached in his pocket for his wallet and to his surprise, the wallet was gone.

"That's funny," he said, turning to Mrs. Parmer, "I was going to square myself with you for your kindness, but I can't find my money; I'll go back up to my room to see if I left it there," and he went upstairs.

He hadn't been gone only a few minutes, when he came back all excited and said:

"It ain't up there either; I'm sure I had it last night before I went to bed, though."

With that he left, saying as he went out, that he would go to see Cale about it.

He walked straight down to Rockwell's place and finding Cale in the barn he informed him about the loss of his wallet.

Parmer acted surprised and asked him how much money had been in it.

"Oh, a couple of hundred dollars and some receipts."

"You might have lost it on the way to my place last night. Did you look for it on the way down?"

"Yes, and it's gone," retorted Corning, as he turned to go, and left Parmer standing there.

Corning didn't know what to do. It was quite a predicament to place a man in, to find himself penniless in a strange town. He hadn't the least idea what course to pursue, when presently he happened to think of the two farmers he had met on the next farm the day before. They had made a favorable and lasting impression on him.

So he betook himself to their place, finding both father and son in the yard, getting ready for their day's work in the field.

After they had exchanged greetings, Corning stated the cause of his visit, omitting nothing and asked their opinion.

"If I were you," John advised, after hearing of his loss, "I would go and see the sheriff, 'cause this ain't the first time that's happened at Cale Parmer's house, according to all reports."

"Yes, and that ain't all," spoke up Josh, "it's been rumored around that 'Big Bill' is in cohoots with Cale when he makes a haul like that and he even sends strangers, like you for instance, who are looking for a night's lodging, to the house of mystery, as Parmer's place is called."

The upshot of it was that Josh drove Corning to Sheriff Van Auken's office in Moravia, who upon hearing his complaint, advised him to see a justice of the peace, who lived nearby, procure a search warrant, bring it back to him and he would serve it.

"Couldn't I serve it myself, seeing I'm a deputy sheriff from Richport, Tioga County," declared Corning, showing his credentials to his brother officer.

"Well, it ain't exactly regular, you know, you being an outsider, but I'll deputize you and you can serve the warrant yourself and search the place. Don't go up there till after dark, 'cause you'll find Cale home by then. Yes and you'd better take Josh here along with you, but say, what brought you here in the first place?" inquired the sheriff finally.

"Oh, I came here on a little business matter, I'll tell you about it later. I may need some more help before I go back home," said Corning, as Josh and he left to find the justice who happened to be in.

Corning stated his case, after making himself known, whereupon the judge drew up the warrant.

"I'll give you the warrant but I'm afraid it'll do you no good, cause Cale is a slippery cuss. We have been after him for some time," the justice remarked, as he handed him the legal document of search and seizure.

Josh was ready and willing to accompany Corning.

Acting on the sheriff's advice they waited until dark, before they started for Parmer's place.

As they approached the house, they got a glimpse of Cale and his wife through the window, the former had his back turned so they couldn't see him very clearly.

Answering Corning's knock, Mrs. Parmer came to the door, inquiring who was there. She opened the door, after Corning made himself known and the two men entered, to find only Mrs. Parmer in the room with her two boys. Of Cale, not a sign.

Yet both of them were positive they had seen him not over five minutes before.

Upon Corning inquiring for her husband, Mrs. Parmer told him that he hadn't come home yet and sometimes stayed over night at Rockwell's.

Producing the search warrant, at the same time showing his badge, Corning then told her that it was his painful duty to search the place.

"Go ahead and search," she answered, just as unconcerned as though it were an every day occurrence. They searched all through the house, up-stairs and down, thoroughly and persistently, yet no trace of Corning's wallet or of Cale Parmer either, could they find.

As the two men returned to the living room on the first floor, Josh happened to notice a small closet in one corner and nodding to his partner, he started towards it.

Mrs. Parmer whose eyes had lit up with triumph as the men had re-entered the room empty handed and who was watching their every move, forestalled him and exclaimed: "That's just a clothes closet, you won't find anything in there, only dirty clothes."

Josh brushed her to one side and opened the closet door, fully expecting to see Cale Parmer step out. After one look inside he motioned to Corning, who joined him quickly. Finding a ladder inside reaching down to the cellar bottom, they both descended. They had provided themselves with a lantern, anticipating just such a contingency.

Following a careful search of the cellar which revealed nothing to our friends, they were about to give up, when Josh walked over to a cupboard built against the cellar wall. The lower door stood open. He got down on hands and knees and started to crawl inside. He backed out of there shortly and motioned to Corning, who was dumbfounded when he saw an opening in the cellar wall large enough to admit a good sized man.

It proved to be the entrance to a tunnel. He crawled in there, while Josh remained on guard in the cellar. The tunnel led in a straight line for about one hundred feet when it ended abruptly in an old abandoned well.

The well was circular in shape and laid up of stones, with iron hooks fastened to one side, forming a ladder to the top of the well, which had a wooden cover over it.

The well was empty and the bird had flown.

Mrs. Parmer was waiting for the explorers as they returned to the living room via the closet route and with a sneer on her face, she inquired what they had found.

"More than we bargained for," Corning responded quietly, "but we were too slow for the pair of you."

Our friends then left for the Rosecamp home to report their

Cale Parmer's House—Cross Indicates Secret Tunnel Leading to Well

findings to old John, who, upon hearing of their failure, exclaimed: "Worse and worse. If this keeps on much longer, we'll have to take the law in our own hands."

Corning had supper with the Rosecamp's, after which the men sat and smoked, discussing their latest adventure.

Ellen, Josh's sister, who had been a close listener to their story, remarked: "I always heard that Cale was a bad one, but I never suspected he was as clever as that. All I've got to say, birds of a feather flock together; meaning Parmer, that 'Big Bill' Rockwell and my good-for-nothing husband."

In the course of their conversation, Corning apprised them of the fact, that he had been sent to Moravia on a mission by the farmers of Richport, Tioga County, who had lost horses in a mysterious manner of late.

"Of course, we always mistrusted 'Big Bill' when he lived among us, but we never could catch him with the goods, so since we have been losing horses right along after he left, they sent me up here to investigate on the quiet, but I'll be dinged if I could find a horse that fits these descriptions." He then produced a list of stolen horses with their owners' names.

"You're just a few days too late, 'Big Bill' stole a march on you," Josh explained to him. He then went on and told all that had taken place since "Big Bill's" advent among them, including the affair at the gully.

Corning left that night, after exacting a promise from Josh, to let him know directly if Rockwell left on another trip, and also advised him to put somebody on his trail in case he did.

In return, Corning agreed to send word to Josh just as soon as any more horses would be missing from his neighborhood.

Before they parted, Corning confided to our friends that he would stop at Moravia to make a report to Sheriff Van Auken, whom he told practically the same story, upon his arrival there, later in the evening.

His parting words were: "Well, Van, I see 'Big Bill' is still too wise to be caught."

CHAPTER X

The Doctor Gets a Warning

DOCTOR WILLIAM COOPER resided in the hamlet of Kelloggsville, about seven miles from Moravia. He was a cousin of the famous James Fenimore Cooper, author of "Leatherstocking Tales."

Past middle age, above medium height, and possessed of a charming personality, the old country doctor was respected wherever he went. Dr. Cooper was a prominent man in the community, highly esteemed by his fellow citizens and he was considered one of the best physicians of the state.

He was a friend of the Rosecamps and used to stop at their place frequently, to see Josh in particular, to whom he had taken a great liking.

They would talk politics and discuss the topics of the day, Josh being a self-educated and highly intelligent young man, besides being a close observer and student of human nature.

One of Ellen's children was taken sick one night and her brother Josh, drove to Kelloggsville after Dr. Cooper early in the morning.

When Josh arrived there, the doctor was out and his housekeeper, an elderly woman, took the message. Josh went back home and after waiting all forenoon in vain for the doctor to come, he drove to Kelloggsville again in the afternoon.

Finding the doctor in this time, Josh stated his errand and asked why he hadn't answered the call.

Dr. Cooper looked up in surprise and replied: "Why Josh, I didn't get any message to come to your place. How could I know that someone was sick there?"

"Didn't your housekeeper tell you that I was here and left a message for you to come to our house as soon as you returned?"

"How could she," replied the good doctor. "When I got home

31

after visiting my patients, I found my housekeeper dead on the kitchen floor."

The poor woman had died of heart disease while Dr. Cooper was out making his daily calls.

The doctor went back with Josh to take care of Ellen's little girl, who had a mild attack of measles.

It was about this time that Rockwell's wife was taken sick and "Big Bill" went to Kelloggsville after Dr. Cooper, who came back with him to attend his sick wife.

The two men who had met once or twice in a casual way, had a profound respect for each other as is often the case with strong minded people.

After making a number of calls and treating Mrs. Rockwell, whose ailment was not serious, the doctor pronounced her cured, but he told Rockwell not to call on him in a similar case.

It happened that Mrs. Rockwell required medical care on another occasion for a disorder of like nature. "Big Bill" did not go after Dr. Cooper this time, mindful of the doctor's ultimatum at the time of his first visit. Instead, he laid for him, watching the main road, knowing full well that the doctor passed by his place quite frequently. He was rewarded for his vigil when he saw the doctor driving along the road presently.

"Big Bill" went out, hailed him and asked him to come in the house to attend his sick wife.

The doctor repeated his former statement, remaining firm in his refusal, whereupon Rockwell suddenly pulled a gun out of his pocket, pointed it at the medical man and threatened to shoot him unless he complied with his request.

Dr. Cooper, taken completely by surprise, gave in gracefully and followed "Big Bill" in the house. Having treated Mrs. Rockwell, the doctor started to leave, when "Big Bill" threw a handful of silver coins on the table, telling him at the same time to take it and get out, which the doctor promptly did, after taking only what money he considered justly his own for his services.

Dr. William F. Cooper, Cousin of James Fenimore Cooper

From that time on Dr. Cooper was a marked man and he knew it.

It was brought home to him very forcibly, shortly after he had treated Mrs. Rockwell under compulsion.

Cale Parmer and Brow Scott came to his office late one night and asked him to come to Lafayette Howatt's place immediately, claiming that Howatt was a very sick man.

Howatt lived in an isolated spot in a lonely part of the country, as the doctor knew well. As it was quite late in the evening, he refused to go. Besides he had his misgivings. Upon inquiry on the following day, he learned that Howatt was as well as ever, in fact that he hadn't been sick at all.

He surmised, and with good reason, that the whole affair had been a ruse to lure him to a certain unfrequented place, selected beforehand, to do away with him.

His suspicions proved to be well founded when, a few nights later, as he was seated in his living room, reading, someone shot at him through the closed blinds, the bullet missing him by inches.

In order to protect himself and by reason of the attempt on his life, Dr. Cooper would have been justified to report his case to the sheriff at once, but he reasoned otherwise, deciding to take his chances. He was a brave man and absolutely fearless like many others of his time. However, to guard himself against night prowlers around his home, who might take an occasional pot shot at him, he went to Prison City and bought a good watch dog. He also procured a gun which he kept within easy reach at all times.

He seldom went out at night after the dastardly attempt on his life. When he did he was accompanied by his great dane and well armed besides.

CHAPTER XI

A Temperance Meeting

THE Moravia House in the village of Moravia was quite a pretentious hotel in its day. It was the best known hostelry for miles around.

A large three-story frame building, with a bar and dining room on the first floor and a commodious dance hall on the third.

All the guest rooms were on the second floor.

The young people of the village and surrounding towns used to hold dances there regularly and some very enjoyable times were had by all.

Entertainments of all descriptions, as well as political and other meetings were held at the hall, it being the only available meeting place the town possessed.

The prohibitionists of that locality, the country was blessed with them even in those days, announced a meeting would be held in the hall on a certain date. A prominent temperance lecturer had been secured for this occasion.

The hall was filled to overflowing, young and old being present.

Rockwell was there, as were Josh and his father, his sister Ellen, and Lu, his sweetheart.

The lecturer, after a scathing arraignment of the saloon in general and strong drink in particular, followed by an eloquent plea for temperance, proceeded to illustrate his lecture, by showing the evil effects of liquor on the human system.

A pitcher of water and a glass were placed on a table before him. He poured some water from the pitcher into the glass and then passed the glass, along with a small microscope, around in the audience. Picture the wonder and amazement of the simple minded country folk, when looking through the microscope, they saw the water alive with wriggling and twisting shapes of all kinds.

After all who wished, had viewed the strange spectacle in the glass, it was handed back to the lecturer, who then called for a glass of liquor. A small glass of whiskey was produced, a few drops of which he poured into the glass of water. Lo and behold, almost at once all organic life in that glass of water became extinct and all the wriggling and squirming ceased.

All those grotesque shapes, alive but a minute before, had stretched and stiffened out.

He then passed the glass back to the audience again, telling his hearers to observe closely the destructive effect of liquor on living organisms. He then went on to draw a parallel, explaining to them that if liquor would destroy animal life, it would produce the same effects on the tissues in the human body. In other words it would destroy the lining of the stomach.

The large assemblage was awed and a deep silence ensued. One could hear the proverbial pin drop. The simple minded town folk were nonplussed.

It was a great relief when the silence was broken by an audible whisper, coming from an old Irish couple who were seated in the rear of the hall.

"Say Pat," whispered Maggie, "hereafter whenever I drink a glass of water, I'll take a drink of whiskey right after."

Maggie didn't relish the idea of her stomach being turned into an aquarium.

The tension was released amid great cheering.

The object lesson which the lecturer had been trying to impress on the minds of his listeners, had been completely lost on the old couple.

After the lecturer had finished and order was restored, Rockwell, who was seated on the speaker's platform, along with other prominent temperance advocates, arose to address the meeting.

Even in those days prohibition and hypocrisy were synonymous. In those days, as well as in our time, one had but to profess to be a prohibitionist, in order to be above reproach.

Like the lecturer, who preceded him, Rockwell also made a strong argument against the use of liquor and he cited his father's example as a warning to others.

Cries of "Shame!" were heard in the audience and the chairman had to rap for order, but "Big Bill" stood there as bold and defiant as ever. Temperance was his one redeeming feature, yet he never attended any church.

After Rockwell had finished, Josh Rosecamp stepped forward, asking permission to address the audience, and the floor was granted to him.

His ire was aroused when his arch enemy, Rockwell, known to him as the embodiment of evil, had the audacity and nerve to address a meeting of respectable citizens. In a fiery speech he took issue with "Big Bill," picturing him as a wolf in sheep's clothing and using such expressions as hypocrite and fakir.

Josh then went on to ridicule the temperance lecturer in the eyes of the people, characterizing him as a narrow minded egotist. He appealed to the good sense of his townsmen. He showed them conclusively that liquor, if taken moderately, is beneficial, rather than detrimental to the human body and that a certain amount of liquor is required by the human system.

"Why, even your physicians will prescribe alcoholic stimulants in certain cases," Josh finally concluded.

Never had his friends and neighbors heard Josh talk like this before and he was applauded to the echo.

Josh was a well read and self educated young man and while he had spoken at different political meetings, he had never waxed as eloquently as he had on this occasion.

The assembled countrymen were aroused as never before and they all but drove the luckless lecturer out of the hall and out of town.

Threats against Rockwell also were heard on all sides, but he left the hall silently and swiftly.

CHAPTER XII

Luella's Advice

JOSH took Lu home after the meeting at the Moravia House that night, his father and sister Ellen having left earlier. Their thoughts naturally turned to Rockwell and Josh was not surprised, in fact he welcomed the question, when Lu asked him what he thought of her employer.

"I was going to ask you the same question myself, before now, but I was trying to find out more about the man 'ere I did," said Josh. "He certainly is a deep one and a clever rogue in the bargain."

"Do you know, Josh, I sometimes feel afraid of him?" Lu continued. "You should see the company he keeps, I mean the men that call on him some nights. Men that I've never seen before; they certainly don't belong around here. They all call him 'Big Bill' and they seem to know each other purty well. When he has those kind of visitors call on him, they all go down cellar to talk. You know the cellar is divided in two parts. One is under the main part of the house, the other under the addition, or wing. A door leads from the front cellar to the one in the rear and a small opening with a trap door over it, leads outside from there. Rockwell always takes his friends down cellar through the kitchen, but they never come back that way. He must let them out through the trap door in the rear.

"I went down cellar after apples one night when he had his company down there. The door between the two cellars was closed, and as much as I listened, I couldn't hear a word they said. They probably heard me coming and lowered their voices.

"Rockwell is good to his family though, and he treats me like one of the family, too."

"He'd better," said Josh, who had been a patient listener to Lu's recital. He was debating with himself that very minute

39

whether or not he should make Lu acquainted with the incident at the gully on that eventful night.

Thus far he had refrained from so doing, for the reason that she would only be needlessly alarmed, and might unintentionally give him away. He could not afford to be hampered in his movements by anyone just then, not even by his sweetheart.

In the end he decided to tell Lu everything.

William Rockwell's Homestead

Being a self possessed girl with a well balanced mind, Lu betrayed little or no emotion when he repeated his unusual experience at Hewett's gully and also his adventure at Cale Parmer's house, together with Corning.

The only time Lu displayed any feeling was, when she begged him to watch out and take care of himself.

"You know Rockwell is a dangerous man. Remember how he treated Dr. Cooper," she reminded him.

Josh promised her that he would be on his guard. Also he requested her to let him know immediately if anything out of the ordinary should take place and to keep him informed in case "Big Bill" made preparations for another trip. After a fond embrace and a kiss to seal their compact, they parted.

On his way home, Josh's thoughts turned to the future, he realized for the first time that he had some grim work cut out for himself, if he would fight their new neighbor to a finish.

CHAPTER XIII

A Grand Old Man

UNCLE WILSON, as he was called by old and young alike, was a kindly old gentleman. He owned the farm next to Rosecamp's, where he had lived since the day of his birth.

His farm lay on the highest point of the plateau on which both Rockwell's and Rosecamp's farms were located.

From his place the plateau sloped both to the East and West, forming a divide.

Uncle Wilson was liked by rich and poor alike. A former sheriff and justice of the peace in turn, he was well versed in the law and had settled many a dispute between his neighbors.

How he got the name of "Uncle" bestowed upon him, no one seems to know, unless it was on account of his amiable and friendly disposition. He was known and respected throughout the state, and although of humble origin, he counted some of the most distinguished men of that time among his friends. Possessed of a wonderful physique, Uncle Wilson was known as the strongest man in the Finger Lakes region. He was endowed with phenomenal strength. Many an unruly citizen had been subdued by him, yet he never boasted of his extraordinary powers. If anyone ever deserved the title of superman, Uncle Wilson certainly would.

Josh would often visit Uncle Wilson, who took a fatherly interest in his young neighbor and who keenly enjoyed his company.

Men from all walks of life used to call on Uncle Wilson for advice. He could hold most any political office he chose, but he declined them all.

Being of a modest and retiring nature, he preferred to live a quiet and simple life, surrounded by his friends and neighbors, and among his native hills.

43

CHAPTER XIV

A Meeting at the Vineyard

ABOUT a month after his adventure at Hewett's gully, Lu made her appearance at Josh's home early one morning, which was an unusual thing for her to do.

Josh saw her coming and noticing her excitement, he went out to meet his sweetheart, who told him she had some important news, concerning Rockwell.

After Lu had regained her composure, she told him the following story:

"Two strange men came to the house last night and Rockwell took them down cellar as he always does with strangers. Not finding any suitable excuse to make it possible for me to go down cellar, I went outside and walked around the house to the little trap door in the rear, hoping to overhear some of their conversation, but without any result. After a long wait, my patience was finally rewarded when the two strangers crawled out through the trap door.

"Imagine my surprise on hearing one of the men exclaim:

" 'Tomorrow night at the Vineyard then, around eleven o'clock.'

" 'Yes and be sure to bring the horses and come prepared for a long trip—we're going to Oneida County,' was Rockwell's reply, as his two visitors vanished in the dark."

The vineyard was a piece of meadow land, about three acres in extent, surrounded by bushes and scrubby trees—a regular clearing in a forest, shut in from all sides. It was seldom visited by anyone and was considered no man's land. Nobody worked it, nobody claimed it. It remains so to this day.

The vineyard lay in the rear of Jim Hewett's and adjoining Rockwell's place.

Lu asked Josh what he intended to do, after she had told him the news of the night before.

"Well, Lu, father ought to know about this and we should also tell Uncle Wilson, who will be greatly interested.

"If I have my way about it, we'll go to the vineyard tonight and surprise the gang, but of course as long as there are no horses reported missing, we're powerless to act.

"However, I'm going to find out where they're taking the horses to, if I have to follow them for a week."

"I do wish you would be careful, Josh, you know Rockwell is a desperate character and will stop at nothing," pleaded Lu, placing her arms caressingly around Josh, as if to hold him back.

"Why not notify the sheriff, it's up to him to catch the gang with the goods on, and you keep out of it. Besides, I feel sorry for poor Mrs. Rockwell and the boys. God knows the poor woman has trouble enough without you causing her more," urged Lu with tears in her eyes.

"I'll see you tonight and let you know what we're going to do, and don't you let Rockwell catch you spying on him, or your time in that family will be short," finally declared Josh.

"Oh, as to that, if it wasn't for you, Josh, and to be near you, I should have left the place long ago. Rockwell's been trying to get fresh with me different times," said Lu.

"D——n his hide, if I ever catch him making love to you, his roving days will be over. Just for that, I'll hound him and show him up. I'll have him behind the bars yet," was Josh's rejoinder, before they parted.

After Lu had gone, Josh imparted the important news to his father, who proposed that they go and call on Uncle Wilson to make him acquainted with the latest developments in the Rockwell case, as soon as their stock was cared for.

Accordingly, they set out for Uncle Wilson's place, who was surprised on seeing his two friends at that hour of the day, and more so, after they apprised him of "Big Bill's" latest move. The news did not shock him one bit, for, as he told them, he expected most anything from Rockwell.

"You see, neighbors, there's been queer doings in these parts since 'Big Bill' has settled among us," said Uncle Wilson. "Things that I can't understand myself, or explain to you. All we can do is to watch and wait."

"Our strange neighbor don't seem to do much farming; he is away from home a good deal, yet he seems to have plenty of money at all times," ventured Josh.

"Yes, and about those trips of his," continued Uncle Wilson. "A short time ago I met a feller from Richport, where Rockwell hails from and he told me 'Big Bill' used to lead the same kind of a life there. He said he would be gone for weeks at a time, selling medicine put up by himself, as he claimed, and he'd always come back with lots of money. That he was also a horse trader and it was rumored in and around Richport that he acted as a fence for a gang of horse thieves, disposing of their stolen horses for them. So you see, we got a bad man to deal with."

Considering the time opportune, Josh then told Uncle Wilson the story of his strange adventure at the gully, some weeks previous.

"You did just right, Josh; and your father gave you good advice when he told you to keep the affair quiet. We ain't got evidence enough against 'Big Bill' yet, but he bears watching all right. So Cale Parmer and Brow Scott are in league with him, the dirty skunks. Well, that's all they needed was a leader, and from all accounts, they found the right party," concluded Uncle Wilson.

Our three friends then discussed their coming expedition to the vineyard that night. They considered the advisability of trailing the band in case they made their getaway with the stolen horses, as they had succeeded in doing at the gully.

Josh was determined in his purpose to follow them, should they put in an appearance that night, in spite of all the two older men would say against it.

"Why, don't you see," Josh exclaimed, trying to convince his two elders, "that it's up to me to follow them, because the time is too short to notify our friend Corning in Richport as we agreed. It's almost uncanny and it seems as if we'd been overheard at the time we made our agreement with Corning, in regard to Rockwell. Ordinarily, it would take them two or three days to drive the horses from Tioga County. So they must have them hidden nearby right now. They ain't at the gully this time neither, but so help me, I'll find their other hiding place before long."

Vineyard—Where Rockwell and His Gang Would Meet

The two Rosecamps then left Uncle Wilson, with the understanding that they would all meet at his house after dark, it being the nearest to the vineyard.

After reaching home again, Josh immediately set to work to make preparations for his trip, having decided to travel on horseback. As agreed, our friends met at Uncle Wilson's about ten o'clock that night, and a little later they started out for the vineyard, about half a mile away.

Josh had one of their fastest horses all saddled and bridled, ready to start at a minute's notice. Lu was staying with his sister Ellen, to await his return.

It was a moonlight night and our friends had to be very careful so they would not be observed by the members of the band.

Upon arriving near the vineyard, they concealed themselves in the bushes and dense undergrowth surrounding it. With their nerves strained to the breaking point, they listened for any sound that might come to their ears.

They had not long to wait, when two men, leading a string of horses, entered the clearing from the south side.

Our friends did not know the two strange men, but they recognized "Big Bill" easily, when he arrived a little later.

As at the gully, Rockwell looked the horses over carefully and after giving some instructions, they left the vineyard with the horses, going in the direction of the main road, closely followed by Uncle Wilson and the elder Rosecamp.

Josh had started for home on a run to secure his horse and say good-bye to Lu and his sister.

It was a sad parting; he had to tear himself away from Lu. He hastened to rejoin his father and Uncle Wilson.

Just before they reached the highway, our friends noticed a team of horses hitched to a democrat wagon and a single horse and carriage standing by the side of the road.

Brow Scott stood guarding them.

After giving some further instructions to his confederates, who were tying the horses on behind the wagon, Rockwell stepped into his carriage, seized the reins and started on ahead. The wagon and team driven by Brow Scott, came next in line. The other two men, each one having mounted a horse, brought up the rear.

The nocturnal procession then started off in an easterly direction and men and horses were soon lost to sight. In the meantime Josh had arrived.

As he was about to start out on his dangerous mission, Uncle Wilson handed him a sealed envelope, admonishing him not to open it unless he was badly in need of assistance; in which case he was to hunt up the nearest official and hand him the enclosed letter.

After a fond and affectionate farewell from both his father and Uncle Wilson, Josh swung himself in the saddle and followed the horse thieves, who by this time, had faded away in the distance.

The two old men stood and watched until Josh was also out of sight.

Then they turned around with a sigh, shook hands and returned to their respective homes, each with a heavy heart.

CHAPTER XV

THE PURSUIT

MEANWHILE, both pursued and pursuer picked their way slowly across Cayuga, Cortland, and Madison Counties to wind up at the notorious Loomis Brothers' stronghold in Oneida County. We will proceed to follow them step by step and give the reader a detailed description of the life and history of those notorious outlaws, at the end of our journey. Over little frequented roads, over soggy and marshy ground, sometimes over corduroy roads, our travelers plodded on, Rockwell apparently in blissful ignorance of being followed.

Like a lone scout, "Big Bill" kept well in the lead, selecting the least traveled roads and the most isolated parts of the country. Evidently the country was not new to him. Early in the morning, following their first night on the road, he called a halt near a small creek, where they watered their horses and fed them some of the grain they carried along with them in their wagon.

Josh was handicapped, not having any feed for his horse, for he only carried a few provisions for himself. In other words, he traveled light. He figured on buying supplies as he went along.

The country through which they traveled (they were now in Cortland County) was heavily wooded, the roads being so narrow in places, that the overhanging branches from the trees sometimes impeded their progress.

Later on in the same forenoon, Josh noticed a lone farmhouse some distance ahead. During the night Josh had kept close at the heels of the pack, because they could not see him, while in the daytime he fell far enough behind so he could barely keep them in sight.

He stopped at the farmhouse to procure some provisions for himself as well as some feed for his horse. The farmer, a rough

51

looking customer, seemed surprised to see a stranger in these parts and said so. Josh satisfied his curiosity by telling him that he was going over into Oneida County to look at some horses he intended to buy.

"That's a fairly good looking horse you are riding," said the farmer. "You better not let him get out of your sight, because you are coming to a tough country. Are you with those fellers that jest passed by here?" he asked him innocently. "I didn't see no one ahead of me, and surely nobody's passed me since I left home. Where do you s'pose they're bound for?" Josh then quizzed him.

"Well, I don't know for sure," said the farmer, "but I can give a good guess. You've heard of the Loomis boys in Oneida County; they'll buy all the horses they can git and no questions asked."

Josh professing ignorance, the farmer enlightened him further on the subject, after which Josh thanked him and went on his way.

About noon of the same day, he sighted his quarry again and he trailed them as close as he dared, until nightfall, when he saw the riders dismount and make camp beside the road. Josh did likewise.

They were still in Cortland County, but close to Madison County by now. To their left stretched a swamp which seemed to have no end as far as he could see. To their right, the timber had been cleared off in places, the land lay higher and was evidently used for pasture.

Josh led his horse some distance from the road where he tethered and fed him.

He then unrolled the blanket he carried with him and laid down to rest, to watch and listen. It had grown pitch dark by then and our young friend found himself confronted by a serious problem. Supposing the gang broke camp during the night and continued on their journey. He could not approach them close enough to watch their movements in the dark for fear of giving himself away. If he remained where he was, he might fall asleep and they then would make their get-a-way unnoticed by him. For sleep he must have, after riding a night and one day. Our hero was no Lindbergh.

Suddenly a bright idea occurred to him. He would circle around them and head them off. Then if they should make an unexpected start during the night the tramping and stamping of their horses would surely arouse him. He decided to leave his horse tethered where it was, realizing the fact, that he could not lead the animal over unknown territory, without causing some noise. Besides, he might encounter some fences. Time enough to come back after the horse, in case the band would start unexpectedly. So Josh took his blanket and making a wide circuit around the unsuspecting horse thieves, he stationed himself at a safe distance ahead of them, near an old tumbled down rail fence.

His ingenuity asserted itself once more, when he conceived the idea of erecting a barricade across the road that they must pass. Then they surely must awaken him by their noise, on finding their passage obstructed. Carrying out his idea, he removed some of the rails of the old dilapidated fence, placing them squarely across the narrow roadway. The moon had come up by now and he hardly dared to straighten up for fear of being detected.

Next, to hide himself more securely from their prying eyes, once they found the obstacle placed in their path. For one thing, he must not remain too close to his handiwork. Consequently he hunted around for awhile, until he discovered some bushes, quite a distance from the road, but within hearing distance of the same, according to his own judgment. So Josh finally decided to call it a day, rolled himself in his blanket and went to sleep.

How long he slept, he didn't know, but when he awoke, the sky was beginning to grow light in the east. He arose and moved slowly and noiselessly toward the road to see if his barricade had been removed. He felt relieved, when he found it as he had left it.

His next objective of exploration was the camping place of Rockwell and his men. He could hardly trust his eyes when he found, to his great chagrin, that men and horses had disappeared. He was fully aroused by now, and hastening back over the road as fast as his legs would carry him, in order to secure his horse and follow the gang, when he received his second shock that morning, on finding his horse gone.

Outwitted! Once more Corning's remark struck him with full force: " 'Big Bill' is too wise to be caught!" After due deliberation, Josh decided to go back over the same road that they had traveled over, and accordingly, he started to retrace his steps.

All at once, he happened to think of the packet that Uncle Wilson had presented to him. "Well," he said to himself, "if I ever needed assistance badly, it is now." So he pulled the envelope out of his pocket, opened it, and finding a letter inside, he read as follows:

To Whom it May Concern:

Bearer of this, Joshua Rosecamp, is a respectable and law-abiding citizen, and he is deserving of any help or assistance he may ask for. Any service that you may render him will be appreciated by yours truly   *Uncle Wilson.*

"Well, Uncle Wilson," said Josh to himself, "now is the time to find out how far your influence reaches." The letter inspired him with new courage however and he struck out with renewed zeal and fully confident that he would yet succeed in tracking this tricky fox to his lair. As he walked on, he kept a sharp lookout for any road or path leading off from the one over which they had come, satisfied in his own mind that "Big Bill" would not double back very far.

His deduction proved correct, when, after walking back about three miles, he found a narrow road, no more than a path, leading off to the north. The path followed the edge of the swamp we have described, but Josh had not noticed it when he passed it the first time.

In the soggy roadway Josh easily discerned the imprints of horses hoofs and the tracks of wagon wheels, convincing proof that he was on the right track once more.

Evidently, Rockwell did not deem it necessary to double back very far, before he struck out across country. Being in possession of his pursuer's horse, he snapped his fingers at any further pursuit.

Josh kept plodding on doggedly and with grim determination until late in the afternoon, when he sighted the first human habitation since he had left the main road. He was completely tired out and hungry, not having eaten a morsel of food since morning, when he had consumed the last of the provisions procured of a farmer on the previous day.

He had left the swamp far behind him by this time and the ground was harder, so he could no longer see the tracks he was following. As he was staggering up to the farmhouse, the farmer, a surly looking brute, met him with a shotgun under his arm and demanded to know his business.

"First, I would like something to eat, and if you'll sell me a horse I'll be going along," said Josh.

"Well, you can't have either," answered the farmer, with an ugly leer on his face. I don't feed tramps and I just sold my last horse this morning."

Josh could readily see that it was useless to appeal to the man's better side. He had to deal with one of those hopeless clods one meets up with occasionally, even now, in the backwoods of the North, or in the mountain regions of the South.

"I'll pay for what I get, I'm no tramp;" Josh then told the farmer, who merely shook his head, pointing down the road with his gun, saying "I don't want your money."

Josh knew then that further argument was useless as well as dangerous. He had about decided to pass on, in the hope of finding another farmhouse before night, when a new thought occurred to him.

He turned back to the farmer: "Say, mister, would you mind telling me who you sold your horse to this morning?"

After reflecting for a few moments, the farmer spoke up and said: "T'won't help you any, but I'll tell ye, you can't catch 'em no more nohow."

"Catch what and who?" Josh flung back at him. He was all attention now.

"Why, them fellers what went past here this morning. Lookit here, the big feller give me some real money for my horse and never jawed me down a penny."

As he said this, the farmer pulled a handful of crackling new bills out of his pocket, shoving them almost under Josh's nose. Josh took one good, long look at the money when a broad smile overspread his face.

"You call that good money? Why them are counterfeits!"

Josh was almost sorry for what he had said, on perceiving the look on the other's face. Never in all his life had Josh seen such a diabolical look on a human face. His features were distorted and he was actually gasping for air. Josh fell back a step and watched his vis-a-vis and the gun closely, especially the latter.

"What's that you said?" the farmer managed to sputter, after he had regained some degree of composure. For answer, Josh took some bills out of his own pocket and held them beside the other's money. The latter's new bills were of such crude workmanship that the average person could tell the imitation at a glance.

Even the farmer could see the difference now. At last it dawned upon him that he had been duped. He replaced the money in his pocket and let loose a stream of profanity, such as our friend had never before listened to. Then he walked over to Josh, took him by the arm and fairly hurled the words at him: "You come in the house and eat."

As soon as they had entered the house (there were only two rooms as far as Josh could see) the farmer spoke to his wife, a slatternly woman, who shrank back from him as if in mortal fear: "You fix this man some vittels d——n quick, we're in a hurry."

Then addressing Josh, he said: "Young feller, as soon as you're done, me and you is goin' to travel." While Josh was consuming his meal, which consisted of the coarsest and plainest fare imaginable, the farmer related his experience of the morning to him. He revealed to Josh that Rockwell had warned him against a young man of his description and to look out for him if he came along, as he was a horse thief. Now Josh could understand the farmer's hostile attitude.

It appears that Rockwell broke camp shortly after midnight. He had been aware of being pursued almost from the very outset. When Josh blocked the road he played right into his hand. It gave him a chance to shake off his pursuer most effectively. Only instead of following the route mapped out by him beforehand, namely from Cayuga to Cortland, to Madison and Oneida Counties, he altered his course and traveled north in Cortland County to Onondaga, to Madison and Oneida Counties.

Taking Josh's horse, was another strategic move on "Big Bill's" part, inasmuch as it prevented his tireless enemy from following him. To cap the climax, when he arrived at the farmer's house on the cross-road at about two o'clock that morning, he bought the only available horse the poor rube possessed, besides his heavy work team. He figured and he figured correctly, that Josh would pick up his tracks, follow to the nearest farm, procure a horse at all hazards and take up the chase where he had left off.

By the time Josh had finished his meal, the farmer had his team hitched to a light wagon and was anxious to start. "Where do you intend to go in that outfit?" Josh could hardly repress a smile as he asked him the question.

"Why, after that crook, where do you 'spose?" and he beckoned to Josh to come. He also had his gun on the seat with him.

"If we go, said Josh, we'll never catch up to them, but we might meet them coming back, if they were foolish enough to return over the same route, which they are not."

It was then that Josh told his newly acquired friend of the

part that he had been playing in this drama and of the loss of his horse. It was comical to watch the simple minded yokel while Josh was telling his story. He simply stared at the latter open mouthed. "Now, let me make a proposition to you, my friend: You drive me to the nearest place where I can buy a good, fast horse, or to the nearest sheriff or justice of the peace. I think it will help us both."

"DeRuyter's the only place I know around here where you kin find one of them fellers, but I ain't a hankering for to meet 'em."

"How far is it from here to DeRuyter?" then inquired Josh.

"Oh, 'bout six or eight miles, I don't just know which."

"How long would it take you to drive there?"

"Two or three hours."

"Well," said Josh finally, "seeing you don't like to meet the representatives of the law, maybe you can tell me where I can buy a good saddle horse around here."

The farmer scratched his head and after due deliberation he replied: "There's Jed Thomas, 'bout two or three miles from here, he might sell ye a good horse if ye don't ask no foolish questions."

"Will you drive me there?" queried Josh, who began to have his misgivings about the country he got into, and who was anxious to be gone and resume the chase. He craved for action. He was like a dog held back in leash.

"You bet I will."

"Let's go, then!"

So they started out in the lumbering old rig, drawn by a pair of superannuated dobbins, who moved at a snail's pace.

They arrived at Jed Thomas' place just before dark, finding him at home. After considerable persuasion and a whispered conversation between the farmer and Jed Thomas, who didn't seem over anxious to deal with a stranger, Josh succeeded in buying a fairly good horse for one hundred dollars. Jed Thomas, a crafty looking young man, who reminded Josh somewhat of his tricky brother-in-law, Brow Scott, drove a hard bargain. Josh soon convinced him that he himself was some judge of horse-flesh.

While this newly purchased animal could not compare with his lost horse, he had to make the best of it. Our hero found himself in the same position as a certain British king, who offered a kingdom for a horse.

Before they parted, the farmer gave Josh a good description of his horse, Josh promising him to keep a sharp lookout for it, and he also agreed to notify the sheriff in regard to Rockwell's fraudulent action. Josh thanked the farmer and handed him a bill for his services, but he refused to accept it. He had a pro-found respect for Josh, but he had seen all the paper money he wanted for one day. After all, there is some good in every man. They shook hands all around and our young friend was in the saddle once more and just as determined as ever to follow the "Terror of the Finger Lakes" and run him to earth.

DeRuyter lies on the boundary line between Cortland and Madison Counties and only a few miles from Onondaga County.

Josh arrived there about ten o'clock that night, and had no difficulty in locating Sheriff Al Cross, who happened to be in town that night on some other business. He stated his case to him, before showing him Uncle Wilson's letter. When Josh noticed that the sheriff didn't seem to take much interest in his case, probably accepted his story with a grain of salt, he pro-duced Uncle Wilson's letter and handed it to him. The sheriff read it carefully. After he had finished, he looked Josh over from head to foot, handed him back the letter and said: "Well, my lad, how well do you know Uncle Wilson?"

"As well as I know my own father; we're his nearest neigh-bors," replied Josh.

The sheriff then shook hands with Josh, who received the heartiest handshake of his young life right then and there.

"We'll go out and get something to eat now and if you are in condition to ride, we ride to-night."

Josh thanked him and assured him that he had slept only too

well the night before. "I am anxious to start at any time, sheriff. I wonder if you could find a better horse for me than the one I've been riding?"

"We'll have the fastest horses in this county, my lad, and from any other county, as we proceed on our journey." The sheriff continued: "I should really take one of my deputies along with us, but three men riding together will arouse suspicion, where two will pass unnoticed. From what you've told me, I take it, that our man is headed for the town of Sangerfield in Oneida County, where the Loomis boys live. We know they're dealing in stolen horses, but so far we've been unable to catch them. Of course, we don't know which way they traveled after you lost their scent, my lad, whether they went through Madison County, which would be their shortest cut, or though Onondaga County.

"That reminds me," the sheriff went one, "there's a man over near Pompey in Onondaga County name of Hi Woodness, who, according to the report sent to me, is one bad hombre. He is not only light fingered, but a fence for stolen goods as well. It is just possible that Rockwell knows him and has stopped off there. No harm to look him up."

Having decided on their course, the sheriff and our young friend started out about midnight to take up the trail of the fleeing band once more.

Riding all that night, they found themselves well into Onondaga County and nearing their first objective at daybreak. They were nearing Pompey, the country was hilly, consequently their progress was slow. The home of Woodness was located in a hollow about a mile from any traveled road and it was by the merest chance that our two friends discovered it.

Hi Woodness was known to all his neighbors as a desperate character, and it was the general belief that he was linked in with the Loomis brothers. His place had been raided repeatedly but no incriminating evidence had been found against him. Yet horses and cattle continued to disappear in a mysterious manner, and the finger of guilt pointed strongly to Hi.

People had seen strangers leave Hi's place with horses in the dead of night. The baffled farmers had about decided to use desperate means to rid themselves of Hi Woodness, when the civil war broke out. Hi joined the forces of the North and was soon swallowed up in that tremendous conflict. That was the last heard or seen of Hi Woodness.

Woodness, a slinking, cringing cur, met them at the door and refused to give any information until Sheriff Cross produced his badge. Even then he denied all knowledge of Rockwell and his men, or of having seen them.

A surprise was in store for our friends, when, on examining the horses in his barn, they found one that fully answered the description of the poor farmer's horse, which Rockwell had purchased with bogus money. Woodness refused to tell how he came by the horse, but when the sheriff threatened to arrest him, he owned up that he bought it of a horse trader the day before. He was willing to release the animal, rather than to come in conflict with the law. Not wishing to be burdened with an extra horse, the sheriff told Woodness to hold it until his return when he would settle the matter.

They were off once more. As soon as they got under way, the sheriff said to Josh: "Well, my lad, I suppose you know that I have exceeded my authority, having no jurisdiction in any county, excepting my own, but I took a chance. We'll soon cross over into Madison County, from there to Oneida County. Once we're in Oneida County, I'll have to make myself known to the sheriff, to have him co-operate with us, which he will, because Uncle Wilson's letter will be respected and obeyed by every officer in the state. The first thing we want now, is something to eat, as well as some rest."

"We'll stop at the next village and get both. A few hours won't make any difference now, because we can't finish our trip to-day. Besides, we can't catch up to the gang no more."

They continued on their journey until they came to a hamlet, where they rested for a few hours. From there they rode to Morrisville, half way across Madison County, arriving there late in the afternoon. After some refreshments and a few hours' sleep, they left Morrisville on the last lap of their long ride, hoping to reach Waterville in Oneida County sometime that night.

They rode into Waterville in the early hours of the following morning, proceeding to the only hotel in town to enjoy a long needed rest.

CHAPTER XVI

The Loomis Gang

WE will now leave our friends and join up with Rockwell who was a day's ride ahead of them.

In the forenoon of the third day since they left Moravia, Rockwell drove into the farmyard of the Loomis brothers.

We will leave them there for the present and will now proceed to give the reader a history of the Loomis brothers, the most notorious outlaws of their time in the East. Their history has never been written before, and should prove interesting reading.

All data has been gathered at the scene of their depredations and much valuable material has been supplied by the old settlers of that region. Our Empire State was infested with bands of outlaws in those days: Rockwell and his band in the Finger Lakes region, the Loomis brothers in Oneida County, and the Earl gang in Madison County.

The Loomis brothers were considered the boldest and the most dangerous of them all. There were six brothers of them: Washington, or "Wash" as he was commonly known, Grove, William, Amos Plum, Wheeler and Denio, called the "judge." "Wash" was the oldest and he was recognized as the leader. He was a bright, intelligent fellow and no one ever bested him in a deal.

Four girls, as pretty as pictures, as the natives used to say, whose names were, from the oldest one down: Cornelia, Eclista, Alucia and Charlotte. All picturesque names. The boys as well as the girls lived up to them.

This was the Loomis family, whose deeds in Central New York as the brains and leader of a horse stealing, thieving, counterfeiting gang are as famous as those of Jesse James and "Billy the Kid" in the southwest. Men of ill-repute from all

63

over joined the Loomis brothers and supplied them with stolen plunder of every description.

While the boys were clever enough to keep out of jail, they were accused of nearly every crime on our statute books. All their neighbors knew they dealt in stolen horses. The horses were delivered to them from other parts. The Finger Lakes region through the agency of William Rockwell had been their main source of supply for years. Counterfeiting was one of the charges brought against the boys. While they were caught passing spurious money on various occasions, they could never be convicted for counterfeiting. The story of the Loomis family really has no beginning and no end. Yet it is one of the most interesting and exciting tales of true adventure in this part of the state which has ever been actually lived.

The beginning, which can be selected most happily, is undoubtedly the wooing of Washington Loomis, senior, father of the Loomis gang.

Rhody Mallet lived on a nearby farm and "Wash," senior, went there one day when he was a young man and got into a quarrel with Rhody. The upshot of it was that she sailed into him and came near to giving him a sound thrashing with a churn or some other implement, which happened to be at hand. When "Wash" was ridiculed about his disfigurements the following day, he admitted it and made a prophesy: "I'm going to marry that girl," he declared, admitting that he had come by his wounds at the hands of Rhody Mallet. "By God, if she can fight for her family like that, she would fight for me, too."

It undoubtedly gives an indication that quick, fierce temper, an unthinking courage was inherited by the Loomis boys and played an important part in their lives. There seems to be no question that circumstances conspired to lead the boys into the rough, adventurous, lawbreaking life for which they are remembered. Stretching in front of the three hundred acre farm, which their father owned in the town of Sangerfield, Oneida County, was nine-mile swamp, a fastness in which one was sure to become lost, if he had the nerve to venture into it. The swamp stretched along Chenango creek.

During their youth the boys learned to know the swamp, a veritable labyrinth of shadowy and treacherous paths through great swamps, which undoubtedly cover many tragedies. It was a perfect shelter for those who wished to disappear for a time.

The Loomis gang was and is known as a band of horse thieves, yet they, like Rockwell from the Finger Lakes region who was too smart to be caught, were never caught stealing any horses.

The horses were brought to the farm, the Loomis boys bought them for small sums, concealed them, changed their markings by a clever use of dies and chemicals and sold them. In modern police phraseology, each member of the Loomis gang was a "fence." Everything was fish for their net. Men, who lived by thievery, brought them horses, buggies, harnesses, anything of value which could be stolen, and they disposed of it. There was plenty of indication the brothers engaged in counterfeiting on a large scale. Despite the long period of their reign of terror, it seems evidence could never be secured sufficient to convict them, nor did any of the men who brought them stolen goods, ever turn state's evidence against them.

This is another feature which the Loomis boys and Rockwell had in common. While members of his gang turned state's evidence against each other, when they were caught in the end, none of them would betray "Big Bill."

It was not long before the activities of the Loomis gang became common knowledge and apparently all the thieves in the region turned to them to dispose of their goods; while others, who had been honest, scenting a method of turning an honest penny, would pick up a horse here or there and drive it into the Loomis farmyard, sell it for forty or fifty dollars and learn soon thereafter of its disappearance.

The horses would be driven into the swamp, changed in appearance and when a large string of them had accumulated, be driven to Albany or some other city and be sold for much higher prices than the boys had paid for them. They would be hitched one after another to the tail end of a wagon. The boys would go over the Cherry Valley turnpike to Albany and sell them there. During the Civil War they did a big business. There was a great demand for cavalry and heavy horses ᶠɔr artillery and trucks and they would dispose of them easily.

Because the Loomis boys would buy any kind of a horse and no questions asked, a regular epidemic of horse stealing had set in. For instance, one of their neighbors had a fine mare stolen one night during hop-picking time. He was a young man and was attending a dance, when another young fellow there told him his horse and buggy had disappeared. He ran out of the house in time to hear the mare's hoofs go drumming over the bridge in the hollow. Hastening to his own home, he harnessed another fast horse and started out in pursuit, picking up no less a person than Grove Loomis to go with him in the chase. There was a light frost and the trail could be followed in comparative ease. It ran south and for fifty-five miles the two followed the fleeting mare, finally catching up with the thief and catching the abandoned horse and rig near Pitcher, Chenango County, near the Cortland County line. The mare had made the fifty-five mile trip in five hours.

A peculiar fact in the history of the gang is that all of them died natural deaths except "Wash," acknowledged leader of the family, who was killed during a raid on the place before the final successful banishment of them.

A posse of farmers burned their house down and the family scattered, several of them finally settling down on another farm about four miles from Parish, while others went with Bill Loomis to Higginsville.

On the night of the raid, "Wash" slept in a room on the lower floor. The men tapped on a window and he got right up and came out where they said they wanted to see him. There was a place out in back, sort of a woodshed; they went there and one of the raiders hit him on the head from behind with a sharp instrument. Dr. Wolcott was called, but he said there was nothing to be done for him as he was dying.

Grove, the brother, was given a terrible blow on the head in the same raid which laid bare his skull for inches. Dr. Wolcott attended him also. Grove recovered and apparently continued his activities as ambitiously as before.

Enraged farmers once seized Plum and strung him up to a large maple tree in the yard as a lesson. Before he had strangled, they cut him down.

"I've never prayed, but I'm going to pray now," the old mother said. One of the men in the posse who heard her, said it was the most heart rending prayer he ever heard in his life. Asa Storm, who was sheriff of Madison County at that time, was there. He took Plum to Morrisville, revived him and put him in jail for a term.

One of the most humorous as well as interesting anecdotes in connection with the gang is a story of Bill after he had moved to Higginsville, Oneida County, east of Oneida Lake. Bill's household ran out of meat and Bill had a strong desire for a good piece of beef for supper. So he called a negro who worked on the place and told him that as soon as a canal boat came along (the farm lay alongside the old Erie, now the barge canal) he was going to pick a fight with the man driving the mules. When the owner of the meat market ran out to see it, the helper was to grab a side of beef from the shop and run home with it.

Everything went according to schedule, except that the mule skinner was more husky than Bill had counted on and he had all he could do to hold his own, once the battle had begun. However, he sailed into him fast and furiously, and as it waxed fierce, everyone within hearing distance naturally ran out to see it. The colored man darted into the shop, grabbed a light side of beef and made off down along the canal with it. When the butcher returned to his shop, he immediately noticed the beef was missing. His vocal complaints soon noised the fact of the missing beef around, and a neighbor happened to mention he had seen the man disappearing up the rock cut with it. That was where Bill's farm was located. It was easy to put two and two together, but Bill fed on beef that night and for many days after. No evidence was ever found to connect him with the disappearance of the beef from the meat market.

At another time, an Irish immigrant who had lived near the Loomis place for about six months, was arrested by police at Montrose, Pennsylvania, and charged with stealing a horse. He was identified as having been seen in the Pennsylvania city the time it was stolen. He was taken there and placed on trial. Grove Loomis and other citizens of the town of Sangerfield, went to Montrose to testify in his behalf. Enraged citizens there believed they were members of the same horse stealing gang and discredited their testimony. The jury disagreed and the Irishman was locked up for a new trial, Grove telling him he would make the inhabitants of the city "pay well for every day you're in jail." The final upshot of the matter was that the real thief was located later, the horse recovered and the innocent man was released. He was ill for several months from the effects of his detention in the prison at Montrose. Evidently Grove kept his word, for shortly after Montrose was visited by the most disastrous fire in its history. Even the jail burned down. The origin of the fire was never discovered.

The cleverness of the Loomis boys was remarkable. Tom Spriggs, a prominent lawyer of Utica, who defended the boys in many cases, once said: "We can try a case, but there is no one can plan it like 'Wash' can."

E. B. Goodin, who was then president of the National Bank at Glens Falls, told "Wash" that if he would work honestly, he could make a fortune in a short time. "Wash" had been charged with paying a bill with counterfeit bills on the Glens Falls National Bank. They never got any evidence that he actually had.

Time came, after their barns had been fired and some of their houses had burned down, when the solid citizenry of the country, mostly farmers, could stand the depredations of the gang no longer, and organized an unofficial posse to drive them out. Descending on the house one day when it was still light, they set fire to it. The mother was there, and pathetically, tried hard to save some of the fruits of her many years of labor. She handed out large gallon and two gallon jugs of maple syrup, asking the raiders to place them by the road. They threw them there, smashing every one.

A farmer down the road had a large colony of bees and the consequences soon became apparent. The raiders had to let down the bars of the fence, and those driving by had to make a detour through the fields for several days. A horse going along that road would have been stung to a frenzy, if not killed, by the excited bees. A man walking towards the road from any point in line with their hives, was sure to be hit in the face time and again by bees, heavily laden with the syrup, returning to their colonies.

Nothing could stop the enraged farmers this time from destroying the stronghold of the Loomis gang, and most of them stayed until the house and barns were reduced to ashes. In one part of the burning building the spectators could see the largest assortment of stolen plunder imaginable, going up in flames—harness, saddles, whips, horse blankets, etc.

After the ruins had cooled off sufficiently to allow their explorations, the astounded farmers discovered an underground passage from the house to the nearest barn.

This explained why the members of the gang could never be found in the house, although they would be seen to enter it. That there were secret passages and hidden rooms in the house, the farmers had long surmised. Evidence of a counterfeiting outfit was also discovered in a section of the cellar, separated from the rest by a solid wall of masonry.

The burning of the old Loomis homestead apparently broke up the family at Waterville. Taken altogether, it appears the Loomis family was of unusually intelligent stock with energies, and had they been directed along different lines, would have brought the members success and renown in various fields.

Bill is said to be the only boy who married, although Grove had a common-law wife, whose name was said to be Nellie Smith.

There are probably few direct descendants on the male side, and all the facts gathered in their history seems to bear out the theory that every act beyond the law was committed by the original family of ten.

There seems to be no question the proximity of the great and inaccessible swamp played a direct and significant part in the history of the gang. If it had not been there, success at horse stealing would have been more difficult, would probably have been given up or never started. The boys' intimate knowledge of its fastnesses was undoubtedly a factor in their beginnings of crime. None of the men or women who remember any member · of the family personally, but fails to emphasize their brilliance, attractiveness and great intelligence.

The same holds true of William Rockwell, whose resemblance to the Loomis brothers was a marked one in many respects. They had many traits in common and their methods were almost identical.

Rockwell, like the Loomis boys, had some ideal places of concealment, provided by nature, to aid him in carrying out his bold operations.

There was the gully, the vineyard and the cave. Rockwell's gang was also broken up in the end, as will be shown later, and like the Loomis brothers, he was finally driven out of the country by the outraged citizens.

Rockwell became acquainted with "Wash" Loomis in a most singular way at a fair in Oneida. "Big Bill" was selling some medicine, a certain cure-all for all ills, prepared by himself. Quite a crowd had gathered around him and he was doing a land office business.

"Big Bill" was extolling the merits and wonderful curative powers of his product. "Wash" Loomis, who had been an interested listener for some time and who was then unknown to "Big Bill," stepped up to the carriage where he was holding forth. He handed "Big Bill" a bottle of his own medicine which he had purchased from him a few days before and shouted, loud enough for all bystanders to hear: "Here is your dope, you fakir. It ain't worth a d——n!"

"I know it," returned "Big Bill" like a flash, "it don't work on wood!"

The face of "Wash" presented a study and for a few minutes it looked as if there would be a fight, but he controlled himself and came back at "Big Bill": "Men have died for saying less than that."

"Yes, but not by your hands," snapped "Big Bill."

Again the war clouds threatened, but Rockwell thought discretion the better part of valor and added: "Say, big boy, come and see me at my hotel to-night. I'm staying at the Madison Hotel, we'll talk this over and have it out."

"I'll be there," answered "Wash," and left.

When they met at the hotel that night, each one instantly realized that he had met his equal. They were a well-matched pair, and it would be hard to find two men as masterful and self confident as "Big Bill" and "Wash."

They were drawn to each other, as if by magnetic power, their minds running in the same channel. Their aim and object was to enjoy an easy life at the expense of others, with the least possible exertion on their own part. They spent that night together and it proved profitable to both of them for their future transactions. They became confidential and laid plans which meant success and mutual gain in the future.

Their illegal traffic in horses, as far as Rockwell's part in it is concerned, dates back to this meeting.

Before they parted, "Big Bill" promised to pay "Wash" a visit before he went back to his home in Moravia, which he did.

CHAPTER XVII

ROCKWELL MEETS THE LOOMIS FAMILY

WE left Rockwell and his men as they neared the end of their eventful trip and drove into the Loomis boys' yard.

Both men and horses looked tired, as could be expected, for they had been on the road for two days and two nights. Evidently their coming had been noticed and "Wash" himself went out to meet them. "How are you Bill?" "Wash" called out, as he shook hands with Rockwell.

"It seems good to see you again; I've been looking for you for some time. Did you have a good trip? You got quite a bunch this time, I see. You better come in the house and rest yourself, you must be tired. We can talk business afterwards."

They went inside while Brow Scott and the other two men, assisted by some of the Loomis brothers, took care of the horses.

The Loomis girls were busy about the house and "Big Bill" was warmly greeted as he met them.

"Big Bill" gave "Wash" the wink as soon as they were inside and they went into another room to talk.

"Wash" listened closely as "Big Bill" told him how he had been followed and it tickled him to hear how he had eluded his pursuer.

"But Josh is a spunky little cuss and he might even follow me here," cautioned "Big Bill". "I think somebody tipped him off."

"Even so," said "Wash," "he must be a day's ride behind you, but we better make sure. As far as the horses are concerned, I can hide them so the devil himself can't find them, but you better send your men back as soon as they have a few hours' rest. Not over the same route though; they better go down through Madison and Cortland Counties, the same way

73

you always go. In the meantime I'll have one of my men on the lookout for your party. That reminds me, Bill, do you think it's safe to send your horses to Albany the way they are, or do you think we better change their looks some?"

"Don't worry," replied "Big Bill", "they've been changed so their owners wouldn't know them, and besides they're quite a ways from home now."

Rockwell was quite adept in the practice of changing the general appearance of horses himself and Hewett's gully had witnessed many a transformation in that line.

In describing his trip, Rockwell had mentioned that they stopped off at Hi Woodness' place near Pompey. "Yes, and I left the horse I bought off the farmer with fake money, with him," continued "Big Bill". "You know, 'Wash' I take no chances. Suppose they found that fool farmer's horse with me, in case they followed us."

Hi Woodness' place was a sort of relay station between Rockwell and the Loomis boys; it was also a haven of refuge in case they were hard pressed.

The Loomis girls, having prepared a meal in the meantime, they all sat down to eat. "Wash" offered his company some liquor, which Rockwell promptly refused but Scott and his two partners accepted with alacrity. After the meal Brow Scott and his two partners left the room, while "Wash" and Rockwell continued their conversation.

Scott walked out in the yard, taking stock of his surroundings, this being his first visit to the Loomis place. As he was strolling around, Grove, the second oldest of the Loomis brothers, beckoned to him to come into the barn and he followed him in. "I want to show you something," said Grove,"I can put you in the way of making money faster than by driving horses."

Grove then produced a wallet and showed Scott a bundle of new ten dollar notes.

"Gee," said Scott, "that's more money than I've seen in all my life, how d'ye get it?"

"From a friend of mine in Albany," replied Grove.   "How does it look to you?"

Scott fingered one of the bills and examined it closely. It was really a good counterfeit bill that could be passed in any place outside of a bank. "If you got fifty dollars, I'll give you ten of these notes for it, you can get rid of them easy on your way back."

"Just you wait a few minutes till I see my boss," said Scott then, and he was off to find Rockwell.

They held a whispered conversation after he found "Big Bill," who then handed him some money.

Scott hurried back to Grove and the exchange was made. His men started on their return trip in the afternoon while "Big Bill" stayed on indefinitely. That afternoon "Wash" showed "Big Bill" his method of concealing horses from prying eyes.

The horses were led into the swamp, each one by a different path, so as to make their tracks confusing. Following an irregular, twisting course, they all converged to one point about two miles from where they entered the swamp. At that point the swamp was almost impassable. There was a sort of an island, comprising about one acre of land, almost entirely surrounded by water, forming a moat. The boys had constructed a temporary bridge, by which the island, as it was known to them, could be reached. The bridge was constructed in such a way that it could be put in place or taken down in an incredibly short time. It was composed of planks which would be hidden in different parts of the swamp when the bridge was not in use. The island itself was fringed in with scrubby trees and underbrush, hiding the interior, which had been cleared off by the boys, completely.

As many times as the swamp had been scoured by officers of the law, as well as farmers' posses, intent on recovering stolen horses or other stock, this island retreat had never been discovered. The horses being taken care of, they all went back to the house.

The four girls, all remarkably good looking, were present.

Rockwell wondered, considering their beauty, why they hadn't all been married off long ago. They were all single and living with their mother and brothers, their father being dead. Had they been in other surroundings, their course of life might have been shaped different and instead of being shunned by the young men of the neighborhood, they might have become happy wives and proud mothers. Besides they never knew a mother's loving care.

The Loomis Boys' Swamp, Where They Used to Hide the Stolen Horses

After all, we are all products of our environment. Cornelia, the oldest, a strikingly beautiful girl, dark complexioned like her brother "Wash," whom she closely resembled, showed a deep interest in Rockwell from the start.

"Big Bill" paid her marked attention and they greatly enjoyed each other's company. These two, Rockwell, the man of the world, bland and suave, and Cornelia, the wild flower, thirsting for knowledge and pining for the society of the male, had much to say to each other, as they sat in the old-fashioned parlor and played the ages-old game of hide and seek. The poor girl appreciated good company, their callers were few and for the most part, undesirable. Therefore, Rockwell, the accomplished ladies' man, had a comparatively easy conquest.

In the course of their conversation, Rockwell learned that Cornelia was fond of horseback riding, so he offered her the pick of his string of horses which she thankfully accepted. That afternoon, when the coast was clear and the stolen horses were being assembled for shipment, Cornelia, according to "Big Bill's" promise, made her choice and she chose Joshua's horse. "You got good taste, young lady," commented "Big Bill," as he presented her with the horse. "That's worth a kiss," said the delighted girl, as she threw her arms around Rockwell and gave him a sound kiss.

"Big Bill" was astonished and agreeably surprised when later on she mounted the horse and showed him a lesson in riding. Never had "Big Bill" seen such superb horsemanship, especially by a woman.

Next morning while they were sitting at the breakfast table in a room facing the yard and also the main road, three men came riding into the yard at a smart clip. They rode almost up to the door and dismounted.

"Wash" noticed them first, gave one good look and hissed: "There's the sheriff, hell's to pay now," Taking Rockwell by the arm, he hustled him out of the room and shoved him, not very gently, into a closet in the next room, saying: "Close the door tight, I mean d——n tight." Then he returned to the other room and faced his visitors.

"Joshua, Sheriff Al Cross of Cortland County and Sheriff Asa Storm of Madison County were the three unexpected and unwelcome visitors. Sheriff Storm, who knew "Wash," in fact all the Loomis boys, stepped forward and said with mock serenity: " 'Wash,' meet my friends, Mr. Rosecamp from Moravia and Sheriff Cross from Cortland County."

"Wash," whose temper was not easily ruffled, and who had found himself in many a tight place before, fell in with the situation readily and making a profound bow, he said smilingly: "Right glad to meet you, gentlemen. What can I do for you?"

"Well 'Wash', we're not after you this time, unless you are stubborn and try to shield and protect the party we're after." He went on and told "Wash" all that we have presented to our readers in regard to Rockwell's trip from the time that he left Moravia until he arrived here; also the part that Josh played in tracking down "Big Bill."

"Of course I know, 'Wash,' that we could look for stolen horses on your place till doom's day without finding them—mind you, I'm not saying that the bunch of horses that Rockwell brought here were stolen. All we want him to do is to give us an account of them, and particularly we would like to know what became of this young man's horse. Will you come across, 'Wash,' or do we have to go through your house? We suspect that your friend Rockwell is right in this house now," concluded Sheriff Storm, who had spoken to "Wash" in a fatherly tone of voice, without heat or passion.

"Yes," spoke up Josh suddenly, "if that wasn't 'Big Bill' I seen through the window, why then it was his ghost."

But it was all in vain. "Wash" would not budge. He denied both in turn, either of having any strange horses on his premises or of knowing or having seen Rockwell.

Josh, who had been looking around the room, paying rather scant attention to the conversation, startled them all, when he exclaimed all at once: "Why there hangs "Big Bill's" hat now," and he pointed to a soft gray felt hat with a broad brim, hanging on the wall.

Had a bombshell exploded in their midst, it couldn't have startled them any more. It might have done more damage, of course. Without a word, "Wash" walked in the other room and came back presently with a hat in his hand which was the exact duplicate of the one that Josh had pointed out. Taking the hat down from the wall he walked over to Josh and held both hats out for his inspection. "Well, young feller," he said, addressing Josh, "now come and tell us which is that man Rockwell's hat, as you call him, or maybe you got it marked."

Josh was dumbfounded. In fact they all were. Speech failed him for the moment. It was some relief when "Wash" finally spoke up and said: "We all, I mean my brothers and myself, wear these same kind of hats, maybe not the same size, but otherwise alike, and believe me they are good, serviceable

The Loomis Boys' Homestead

hats. Now, young feller," turning to Josh, "you are so cocksure of having seen this so called man Rockwell in this room awhile ago, now you go find him, the house is yours. If you can tell him as quick as you did his hat, you'll be a long time looking for him, I'm thinking."

"Well, 'Wash,' " spoke up Sheriff Storm, "we've heard about enough of your kidding, we will now give your house the once over."

Accordingly, they passed from room to room. The closet where "Wash" had deposited Rockwell so unceremoniously, was one of the first ones they explored. But no sign of "Big Bill," no hidden ladder either; just a plain closet, with floor, ceiling and sidewalls intact.

Upstairs, through the attic, back down again, in the cellar which underwent the closest inspection of all, without any result. Completely discouraged, not to say disgusted, our friends returned to the living room, where "Wash" awaited them with a grin on his face. Some of his brothers and sisters were in the room with him, not one of them having accompanied the searching party. "We'll go through the barn, but it's only a matter of form," eventually spoke up Sheriff Storm, motioning to his two companions who followed him to the barn.

It was hard to describe the feelings of Josh, who followed them out meekly. He was completely crushed. Again and again, Corning's words kept ringing in his ears: "'Big Bill' is too wise to be caught."

The search of the barn yielded no better result than that of the house and our friends were, to use a modern slang phrase, completely flabbergasted.

There was nothing left for them to do, but to return from whence they came, which they proceeded to do at once.

Josh rode back with Sheriff Cross as far as DeRuyter, where he recovered the horse he had bought of Jed Thomas and had left at the hotel in DeRuyter.

"Well, better luck next time, my lad, and always remember it's a long road that has no turn," Sheriff Storm told him as he bid him good-bye. "Remember me to your father and Uncle Wilson." A few minutes after that, Josh was in the saddle once more and homeward bound after his fruitless expedition.

No sooner were his late unpleasant visitors out of sight, when "Wash" hurried out to the barn, walked over to the haymow, removed some hay from a corner of the mow, exposing a wooden shaft about six feet high with a sliding door near the top, large enough to admit a good sized man. He swung himself inside, grabbed the rung of a ladder, which was fastened to one side of the shaft and let himself down swiftly but surely to the bottom.

Arrived at the bottom, he entered an underground passage, high enough to permit a man to walk in a stooped position. The passage led from the barn to the house or vice versa. After he had covered approximately one hundred and fifty feet, he came to a small chamber and there as complacently as you please, sat Rockwell on a pile of straw.

"Well, Bill, you can come out now, they're gone," he said, laughing heartily.

"Whew!" answered "Big Bill," "that was a close call, I thought I was a goner."

"You had quite a drop, didn't you?" continued "Wash," still laughing. "Come on in the house and I'll show you how it was done."

Arrived in the house, "Wash" went directly to the closet, opened the door and explained to Rockwell the mechanism that precipitated him so unexpectedly on a pile of straw in the cellar. "You see, Bill," elucidated "Wash," "after you stepped in the closet, you closed the door tight as I told you. That released a catch on the under side of the floor, which is really a trap door. You went down through, the floor swung back, propelled by a powerful spring, fastened to the under side of the door too, and you know the rest."

"Yes," said "Big Bill," "I had time to examine the workings of your slide, while I was down there, although it was pitch dark. I got to hand it to you, 'Wash,' you are far more clever than I am and I thought I was some schemer myself; but look here, and this is a horse of another color—I got to leave immediately."

"That cocky little neighbor of mine has got to learn his lesson completely and thoroughly, because I am going to beat him home and give him the ha-ha when he arrives. You saddle the toughest and fastest horse you got, I'll leave my rig here till next time. I'm going to ride," and ride he did.

While the boys got a horse ready for him, Cornelia, who had been hovering near, quietly slipped out and got Josh's horse, presented to her by Rockwell. She had a place of concealment of her own for her horse. She saddled and bridled him and stood there, calmly waiting for Rockwell as he came out. After a hasty farewell from the boys, "Big Bill" swung himself in the saddle, touched his horse with the whip and was gone.

Picture his amazement, when after riding for a few minutes, another horse and rider drew alongside of him, almost forcing him off the road. "Well, I'll be d———d," said "Big Bill" under his breath, as he looked around and beheld Cornelia.

"Say, this won't do, you know," he started to say, when she cut him off with—"Oh, I am only going to accompany you for a few miles, to speed you on your journey."

He was beset by conflicting emotions. At first, he was inclined to be displeased with her conduct, but on second thought he felt sorry for the poor girl, shut out from the world, as it were and denied that, which every girl prizes highest in her life, love and friendship of man. They were a splendid, well matched pair. Rockwell sat his horse like a Buffalo Bill, this mystery man from the Finger Lakes region, while beside him, Cornelia with flowing hair, swept along like Diana, the goddess of chase. How those two could ride.

They fairly flew along, neck and neck, their horses hoofs barely touching the ground. The horses themselves, given free rein, with nostrils extended, shared in the exhilarated feelings of the riders. Truly a glorious ride.

Anyone watching them couldn't help but think that it was an elopement. But all things must come to an end. After riding furiously for about ten miles, "Big Bill" reined in his steed and catching Cornelia's horse by the bridle, they came to a dead stop.

"Well, my girl, you better turn around and go back now, the best of friends must part and we have come to the parting of the ways."

Tears welled up in her eyes as she looked at him pleadingly and said: "I could ride on with you like this, forever, but you know best, it won't do." With that she reached over, pulled his head down to hers and gave him one last, longing kiss.

He reached in his pocket, pulled out a small case and handed it to her. "This is to remember me by," is all he said.

She opened the box, finding a fine gold chain with a locket attached. A diamond gleamed brightly in the center of the locket. Her joy was unbounded, never till that day had the poor girl possessed any jeweled adornment to bedeck herself with.

"Open it," he said coaxingly.

She did so and finding his picture inside, she held it to her lips and kissed it. In another instant she bestowed a kiss on the original of the miniature.

Touching the spurs to his horse, he wheeled suddenly and was gone. He looked back only once, to see her sitting like a statue waving a last farewell at him.

Thus she sat and stared till he was out of sight, when she too turned her horse and rode fast and recklessly back home.

Rockwell made his return trip in less than half the time it took him to cover the same distance with his train of horses. He overhauled his men who had started out one day ahead of him, but he didn't see them, having chosen a nearer route.

Josh returned a day later and as he passed Rockwell's place, jaded and worn, the latter was just coming from the barn. "Well, well, Josh; where have you been all this time?" was his greeting.

"D——n well you know, but I'll get you yet, you slicker," growled Josh, as he rode slowly home.

As soon as his father laid eyes on him, he saw disappointment written all over his face. Shaking hands with him, he greeted him with the words: "Stung again," eh, Josh?" Whereupon his son told his interesting story and reported his failure.

He sure gets all the lucky breaks, my boy, but I think he's about gone the limit and has nearly reached the end of his rope," said old John consolingly.

"As soon as you've had something to eat and have rested up a bit, we'll go up to Uncle Wilson's. He's anxious to see you.

Ellen, who was preparing a meal for Josh, noticed intuitively that things had gone wrong with her brother. In order to cheer him up she told him that Lu had been to the house every night to inquire for him, while he was away.

"I hope she'll come to-night, because I've got a lot to tell her," answered Josh. After he had satisfied the inner man and rested up a bit, Josh felt in better spirits and father and son set out for Uncle Wilson's place.

They found the old gentleman home and after a hearty greeting, Josh proceeded at once to relate his exciting adventure, or series of adventures rather. Uncle Wilson listened attentively until Josh got through, when he said: "So you had another failure and lost your horse in the bargain, eh, Josh? Well, that's too bad. I'll see Sheriff Van Auken to-morrow; we got to rid ourselves of this pest. The funny part of it is, that we ain't heard a word from our friend Corning from Richport yet. I just wonder where they got their horses from this time."

"It strikes me," interrupted old John, "that we have a widespread organization to deal with, with Rockwell as their leader. That explains his peddling trips."

"If we only knew where the Loomis boys ship their horses to, we could cover the other end of their underground railroad, and we might recover some of the stolen horses, and yours too, Josh," spoke up Uncle Wilson. "In the meantime, we'll have to watch closer than ever and sleep with one eye open. I'm right glad that you was well received by Sheriff Cross, my boy. I used to know him well in my younger days and also Sheriff Storm," Uncle Wilson concluded. "I saved both their hides more than once."

Lu put in an appearance that night and the meeting between the two lovers was a happy one.

"Rockwell asked me all kinds of questions about you, Josh, since he got back," said Lu. "He suspects me of giving you information concerning his trip. I got a good notion to leave."

"You better stay awhile longer, right now is the time you are needed on the spot; something is liable to turn up most any time. 'Big Bill' has had all the breaks so far, but things must come our way soon."

And they did. Next morning when Josh went out to their barn to feed the horses, he couldn't hardly trust his eyes when he saw the tails and manes of their best team clipped off close. The team had been all ready to ship to the metropolis and they were to receive a good price for it from one of their best customers. Of course, they were despoiled for the present and they had to ship another team in their place. Josh encountered Cale Parmer some time after that and openly accused him of having committed the outrage.

"I don't know anything about it, but it serves you right. That's what you get for sticking your nose in other people's business and snooping around in their houses," was Cale's cool rejoinder. "Since when are you a deputy sheriff to go and search my premises? It's lucky for you that I wasn't home that night."

"Oh, you was there all right, but we'll git you next time. We'll plug that hole in the wall for you."

With this parting shot Josh left him. That's all the satisfaction he got.

CHAPTER XVIII

A Humorous Incident

MOSE Ally, half-witted, harmless, was a local character. Light hearted, cheerful, he wandered from place to place, getting a day's work here and there. Happy-go-lucky, he knew everybody and he knew "Big Bill," whom he had worked for at different times, doing odd jobs.

Rockwell had an old muzzle-loading gun which Mose coveted, so he asked him one day what he'd take for the gun. "Big Bill" told him he could have the gun, providing he worked for him for one month. Mose accepted the offer and he had been working for about three weeks when "Big Bill" startled him one day by saying: "Say Mose, the sheriff was here to-day, looking for you. What have you done now?"

Mose scratched his head and seemed to be lost in deep thought. Then he turned and left the place, without hearing any more. He was missing from his accustomed haunts for nearly three months, when he turned up unexpectedly at Rockwell's one day, demanding his gun.

"Oh, no;" said "Big Bill;" "you can't have the gun. You didn't stick to your bargain. You didn't work for me for one month as you agreed."

"I allus thought you was a dead beat," was Mose's parting shot, as he left without the gun.

Big hearted and generous as Rockwell appeared to be at times, he would be just as mean and cruel on other occasions.

CHAPTER XIX

LUELLA MAKES A DISCOVERY

LU went out riding with Josh one Sunday afternoon to pay a visit to her parents. On their way home that night they passed two men in a carriage with a pair of horses tied on behind. After they were out of sight of the two men, Lu asked Josh to stop as she thought the horses looked familiar to her and she believed they belonged to Milo Cox, a neighbor of her parents. "There's something wrong here, Josh; we better stop them and find out where they're going. I'm sure the horses belong to Cox and they must have been stolen, because he was offered a good price for them, yet he wouldn't sell. The two men look familiar to me too, but I don't know their names. I think they're some of Rockwell's friends, that call on him nights."

So Josh stopped his horse and waited for the two men to drive up. No men or carriage appeared. They became suspicious, turned around and went back the other way, reasoned Josh. "I think you was right after all, Lu." She had been correct, for Milo Cox reported the next morning that his team of colts had been stolen on the previous night.

The sheriff was notified and he got busy on the case at once. At Josh's suggestion he went to Rockwell, quizzing him in regard to the missing horses. "Big Bill" was very emphatic in professing ignorance.

Following the disappearance of Cox's horses, Josh went out every night to visit the gully and vineyard in turn, fully expecting the stolen horses to turn up at either one of the two places sooner or later.

In the meantime, Lu watched "Big Bill's" every move, ready to report to Josh anything that might furnish a clue to the missing horses. If "Big Bill" was implicated, he gave no signs of it. As a rule he covered his tracks thoroughly.

About a week after their disappearance, Cox received word that one of his colts had been seen in Ithaca, a village some twenty miles from Moravia. He went there and found one of his horses in a livery stable, whose owner told him the horse had been left in his care by two strangers the week before.

Of the other horse no trace could be found. So Milo decided to try an experiment of his own. He untied the colt and drove it out of the livery stable. The frightened animal ran through the streets neighing loudly. As it ran past a livery barn in another part of the village, an answering cry was heard and Cox recovered his team mate.

The identity of the two horse thieves remained unsolved for the time being.

Lu happened to mention in Rockwell's presence one day what Josh and she had witnessed on the night Cox's team was stolen. "Yes, and I'm quite sure I've seen those two men right here in this house," she added.

"You're mistaken, you and your meddling friend; you better keep still about it if you don't want to get in trouble," spoke up Rockwell sharply.

Lu was not to be intimidated, she knew she was right about the two men and she kept a sharp lookout for them.

She was rewarded for her vigilance, when the two men in question came to the house one evening, inquiring for Rockwell, who had gone to the village. Lu recognized them instantly. They left in the direction of the village after being told that Rockwell had gone there. Lu left the house under some pretext or other and hurried to the Rosecamp place, fortunately finding Josh at home. Lu told of her discovery in as few words as possible. Josh hitched up his horse at once and telling Lu to get in the carriage with him, they started out for the village to find the sheriff. They drove to the Moravia house and in the bar room they found "Big Bill" talking to the very men they were looking for—Henry Bates and Charlie Tidd. The sheriff knew them both; so did Josh, after he got a good look at them.

The sheriff asked Lu to point out the men she had seen with Milo's horses on that Sunday night. She positively identified them without a moment's hesitation.

"Big Bill" was inclined to get ugly, but when the sheriff told him to consider himself lucky not to be mixed up in the deal, he tried to laugh it off.

Bates and Tidd were arrested and the sheriff asked Josh if he would guard them for the night. He consented, with the understanding that he would take Lu home first.

The town possessed no jail, so the two horse thieves were locked up in a room in the hotel until Josh returned.

No lockup was required in the peaceful village of Moravia, prior to Rockwell's invasion with his horde of disorderly and law-breaking followers. The population consisted, with very few exceptions, of orderly, law abiding citizens. Josh drove back to Rockwell's with Lu to get her personal belongings, both of them realizing that her presence there would no longer be desired, after what had taken place. It was a sad and tearful parting when Lu bid Mrs. Rockwell good-bye.

The poor woman had lost another good friend and she would again be alone with her ungovernable husband. Lu and she had become deeply attached to each other, but Lu considered it best for herself to leave, because her position would be unbearable after what had taken place.

When Josh returned to the hotel, after he had taken his sweetheart home to her parents, the proprietor installed him and the two prisoners in the dance hall on the third floor, where two cots had been placed for Bates and Tidd, respectively, Josh preferring to spend the night in a chair.

The two prisoners, who acted sullen and dejected, retired quickly, while Josh assumed his lonely vigil. He was reading a book and in spite of all his resistance he fell asleep, to be aroused by a noise near one of the windows. He had no idea as to the time or how long he had slept, but the light was burning low and it was almost dark in the room when he awoke with a start. His eyes searched the room quickly to locate the cause of the disturbance, when, to his amazement, he saw the figure of a man rise up slowly from the floor, near one of the windows and fumble with the lock. By this time he was fully awake and pointing his gun at the shadowy form he called out: "Stay

Moravia House—Cross Indicates Room Where Josh Guarded His Two Prisoners

where you are, or I'll fill you with lead." Walking over to the man, he recognized him as Bates, who stood there motionless, glaring at him.

"Aha, you was going to give me the slip and you almost succeeded. Back to bed for yours, or I'll blow your head off," cried Josh.

The window opened on a three story porch and it would have been an easy matter for Bates to escape, once he got through the window. He could slide down to the ground and to safety by way of the columns.

When the two rustlers were brought to trial, Tidd turned state's evidence, to be pardoned, while Bates got a term in prison.

After his release from prison, Josh met Bates on Main Street in Moravia one day and he was astonished when Bates got down on his knees before him and asked to be forgiven for his wrong doings, begging Josh for a chance to regain his confidence.

Bates felt his disgrace keenly. He had been misled by "Big Bill," like many others. He revealed Rockwell's part in the dirty deal to Josh and he became one of his best friends and staunchest supporters. Through him Josh gained valuable information in regard to "Big Bill's" future plans.

From that time on it was open warfare between Rockwell and Josh. When they met in the road, shortly after Bates and Tidd had been arrested, "Big Bill" openly threatened Josh for interfering in his business and advised him to watch his step or he might get hurt.

"You mean like Dr. Cooper, don't you? Oh, we're on to your game all right, but you've about reached the end of your rope," Josh told him and left him, guessing. A neighboring farmer raised pigs for the market. He had about fifteen on hand when "Big Bill" stopped there one day and offered to buy one. "They're not for sale," said the farmer. Next morning his pigs were all gone.

CHAPTER XX

ROCKWELL IN ANOTHER ROLE

ONE would naturally suppose that Rockwell would have his misgivings and read the handwriting on the wall by that time. Not him, he was just as debonair and carefree as ever and if he felt the net tighten about him, he gave no outward sign. He was a frequent visitor at the Moravia house in the village and although he never drank, he was one of the jolliest of them all and quite a liberal spender.

He happened to be in the bar room of the hotel one evening and there were quite a few of the young bloods from the village present. The conversation turned to the interesting subject—woman. Someone mentioned the name of Viola Allen, a handsome girl of the village, who was considered the belle of the town.

Viola had been wooed unsuccessfully by many a young suitor. No one had been favored by her in particular and the rivalry among the young farmers for her possession waxed keen. Rockwell appeared to be greatly interested in the conversation, concerning the village beauty. When one young fellow solemnly informed him that Viola had spurned the attention of all young men and could not be induced to go out with any of them, "Big Bill" laughed and said: "Pshaw, you fellers don't know how to treat a girl. I'll bet a good supper for all present that I will take Viola out in less than three weeks from now."

He won his bet, for it was only a few days later when he was seen driving through the village streets behind a spirited pair of horses, with Viola Allen beside him. Viola could be seen in his company quite often after that. "Big Bill" owned a boathouse on Owasco Lake, and on many an evening Viola and him would be seen out rowing.

It was whispered by the younger element that "Big Bill" had handed her a love potion, some dope concocted by himself.

"Big Bill" had a way with women and more than one member of the fair sex found it out to their sorrow.

No doubt, Mrs. Rockwell had heard about his clandestine love affair, for news of that character traveled fast, even in those days, yet she never complained. The poor, long suffering, little woman knew the failings of her dashing mate. She was overpowered by his master mind and had long since become resigned to her fate.

Poor Viola paid for her foolish infatuation with her life. The unfortunate girl was drowned in Owasco Lake. Her body was discovered floating in the lake near "Big Bill's" boathouse.

Ugly rumors were afloat at the time, connecting Rockwell's name with the tragedy and the friends of the poor girl laid her death squarely at his door. The wheels of justice moved slowly in those days and no action was ever taken. It was merely another of those tragedies, the result of male persuasion and the penalty for female indiscretion.

CHAPTER XXI

The Chestnut Mare

A VERITABLE epidemic of horse stealing had set in since Rockwell's arrival in Moravia. The terrified farmers got in the habit of locking their stable doors.

Lafayette Hewett possessed a fine chestnut mare. He had received many offers for her, and turned them all down, having no desire to part with the animal. The mare was missing one morning and although Hewett hunted the country over, he could find no trace of her.

A traveling salesman, who was well acquainted with Hewett, stopped at his farm one day to pay him a visit. Incidentally, he told "Lafe" that he knew where he could buy a mate for his splendid mare, being ignorant of the fact that the mare had been stolen.

Hewett became interested at once and asked him where he had seen the horse in question.

"Over in Ithaca, in Master's livery stable," the salesman informed him.

Hewett drove there immediately, and sure enough, he found the mare. Master's description of the man who had sold her to him, did not fit the person "Lafe" had mentally connected with the theft. He suspected "Big Bill" or some of his henchmen.

During this period, Mervin Reynolds, Hewett's hired man, had been spending money freely at the Moravia house in the village and "Lafe" had heard about it in a roundabout way. Reynolds had been seen there with Rockwell much of the time.

Upon questioning Mervin and threatening to call in the sheriff, Reynolds confessed that he stole the mare on the night she disappeared, drove her to Ithaca, disposed of her and was back to work by morning, but he would not disclose how he got back.

"Lafe" tried to have Mervin admit "Big Bill's" complicity in the theft, but he completely exonerated him. Inasmuch as Mervin agreed to refund the money he had received for the mare, "Lafe" dropped the case. So great was "Big Bill's" power and influence over the men who did his dirty work, that none ever welshed on him.

CHAPTER XXII

JOSHUA'S ADVENTURE AT THE CAVE

EVERYTHING was quiet, things had settled down, and life in and around Moravia had assumed its former aspect once more. Peace reigned in the Finger Lakes region. Had Rockwell decided to turn over a new leaf? Did he intend to go straight? Can a leopard change his spots? We shall see.

Lu having left Rockwell's employ, Josh's source of information was eliminated. He was making one of his regular trips to Hewett's gully one night and he had strayed further than formerly.

He was nearing its further, or eastern end, which was about four miles from Owasco Lake. Not a sign of life had he discovered and he was about to go home, when, call it intuition, or call it what you may, as he stood and listened, he heard the faint murmur of voices, coming apparently from nowhere. He walked around in a circle, listening intently, but not another sound came to his ears.

He was about to give up when he detected a tiny shaft of light coming from a crevice of a rocky formation at the side of the gully. Slowly and noiselessly, hardly daring to breathe, he crept towards the little illuminated spot, no larger than a pencil. The light came through a fissure of the rock and now he could hear the hum of voices plainly. He was about to apply his ear to the crack and had squatted down in order to do so, when he felt himself seized from behind in a powerful grip and a hand was clapped over his mouth.

Josh struggled fiercely; he was a strong, rugged young fellow and a wrestler of note, but his captor's grip would not relax. His assailant gave a sharp whistle and the rock was rolled aside from the inside, seemingly by unseen hands, revealing a cave whose existence had been unknown to Josh. He was thrust unceremoniously through the opening and looking around, he beheld five or six men, all unknown to him but one. A lantern furnished the only light. The stone was rolled in place again by two of the men and the entrance was blocked once more.

"Well, young fighting cock, been spying again?" the tallest of the men, who was Rockwell, of course, addressed him. Josh couldn't say a word, he was stunned.

The Cave where "Josh" was Kept a Prisoner

"Fooled again, eh; what are you going to do about it?" the tall man continued. Josh was on his feet now and he made as if to spring at him, but the big fellow waved him back, laughing good naturedly. "We're not going to hurt you, but I'm going to learn you a lesson. Let me tell you something. This is a secret order, we have a right to meet here. This is my property. You came here of your own free will and you shall stay here for awhile," said the big man with a cruel smile on his face.

Up to this time Josh hadn't said a word, but now, speech having returned to him, he said in a level voice: "You hold the trump card again, but I'll get you yet, once I get out of here."

"Why can't we be friends? I have nothing against you, but you have been fighting me ever since I came here," the big man pleaded. Josh only shook his head.

"Well, we must be going," said the speaker, turning to his companions. They removed the stone once more. It took the combined efforts of two of the men to do so, as Josh noticed with dismay, and crawled out, one by one. Rockwell was the last one to leave. Before he went out, he spoke to Josh once more, saying: "If you give me your word, I know your word is good, that you will stop persecuting me, you can go home; if not, you'll stay."

Josh never answered.

"Big Bill" turned and followed the others. After they got outside the cave, they rolled the stone back in place, wedging it tight in the opening and were gone.

Josh was virtually a prisoner. He knew it wouldn't be any use in trying to find a way out that night, so he resigned himself to his fate and sat down on a rock.

When Josh failed to come home that night, his father and sister Ellen became alarmed. Old John went up to Uncle Wilson's place before daybreak the next morning and broke the news to him.

The old gentleman was more agitated than old John had ever seen him before. "If anything happened to Josh, I mean if he has come to harm through Rockwell, I'll throttle that skunk with my own hands," he hissed. "We'll go down to his place right now."

Suiting the action to his words, they started out. There was no one astir when they arrived there. Uncle Wilson soon made himself known by his peremptory knocking at the door.

Mrs. Rockwell came to the door, a timid, shrinking little woman and informed them, upon inquiring for her husband, that he had left the night before, for parts unknown to her.

The two old men went back, dejected and discouraged. Foiled again, "Big Bill" had scored once more.

"Nothing to do now but to organize a searching party," said old John.

"Yes, and I'll drive down to report to Sheriff Van Auken and get some help," replied Uncle Wilson.

A posse was organized. They searched the gully from one end to the other, then the vineyard as well as the surrounding country for miles, but no sign of Josh. Tired out and completely discouraged, Uncle Wilson and old John returned home from their fruitless search at noon.

"Do you suppose he carried Josh along with him to drop him on the way later on?" suggested old John.

"Oh no," replied Uncle Wilson, "he is too wise for that. He won't run any more risks; he had a close call on his last trip, you know. I rather think Josh is being held somewhere until "Big Bill" is beyond pursuit."

Uncle Wilson came nearer to the solution than he anticipated. Rockwell had instructed Cale Parmer to liberate Josh that night in case he wasn't discovered by his friends before that time. He wanted Josh detained long enough to prevent him from trailing him a second time. He had no desire to kill him.

In some way Lu had heard of the disappearance of her lover and she hastened up to Rosecamp's place. The poor girl was almost frantic. It was pitiful to see her suffering. She would not be consoled. She begged and besieged the two men as well as Jack Feek, boon companion of Josh, to do something.

"I've told him to leave Rockwell alone, but he wouldn't listen," Lu kept repeating over and over again.

Suddenly Lu jumped to her feet and shouted: "Oh, why didn't I think of this before. Drive me down to the Cascade house quick, somebody; one of the guests in the hotel owns a bloodhound. When I went there the other day to apply for a position, Martin Smith, the proprietor of the hotel, showed me the dog."

Uncle Wilson drove down with Lu. They found Smith, whom Uncle Wilson knew intimately and the rest was easy.

The owner of the dog offered to go back with them, after they laid their case before Smith. Arriving at Josh's home, Ellen produced some of Josh's garments, so the dog might pick up the scent. The bloodhound was held in leash by the owner and true to his nature he started off, with head down, in a straight line for the gully. Uncle Wilson and old John followed as fast as they could. The owner had all he could do to hold the dog back. He led them a merry chase. Up and down the gully he went, crossing and recrossing it. Sometimes it looked to our friends as if the dog had lost the scent, but always he picked it up again. Every now and then they would stop and listen, expecting to hear a sign of life from Josh, but all in vain.

By this time the dog had led them to the farthest end of the gully and they had about abandoned all hope of finding Josh, when the dog stopped and gave a joyous bark.

The men hollered, calling out Josh's name, and were overjoyed to hear a faint shout coming from behind a huge pile of brush. The gangsters had heaped some brush around and over the cave, before they left the night before, completely hiding the entrance.

The rescuers removed the brush and Uncle Wilson, giant that he was, rolled the stone away alone.

Josh was none the worse for his involuntary confinement.

Lu, who had followed the men, unnoticed by them—they had been intent on watching the dog—then joined them.

The meeting between the two lovers was pathetic in the extreme. Lu had given Josh up for dead, knowing the desperate character of "Big Bill" and his hatred for Josh.

Our friends went inside the cave to examine it. It was large enough to accommodate a dozen men and high enough to stand upright in it.

Josh related to his listeners how he got trapped and described his captors who were all strangers to him but Rockwell. He was filled with a boiling rage and spoiling to follow his enemy once more, when he was informed that Rockwell had gone on another trip.

"No use, Josh;" counselled Uncle Wilson, "he's got too big a lead this time and when he's hard pressed, he's got more holes to duck into than a fox. It beats me, here we have lived in this section all our lives and never knew of the existence of this cave. 'Big Bill' hasn't been here a year and he discovers it. Wonder who tipped him off. Hewett, possibly. I wonder."

They returned home, thanking the owner of the bloodhound for his timely assistance.

On that same day, Deputy Sheriff Corning arrived from Richport.

He reported to our friends that quite a number of horses had again mysteriously disappeared from their section of the country. Our friends then told Corning that he was just one day too late, as he had been on a previous occasion.

After Corning had heard about Josh's capture at the cave on the night before, he was like a wild man, and threatened to shoot "Big Bill" on sight.

"Take it easy, my boy," spoke up Uncle Wilson; "I'll take care of him myself, as soon as he comes back this time. Why, you couldn't even arrest him unless you caught him with stolen horses." Our friends then acquainted Corning with Josh's eventful chase after Rockwell and his band from the vineyard. Corning was speechless and when he finally found words, he exclaimed: "That's beyond me; is he man or devil? 'Big Bill's' too wise to be caught is right, I guess!"

Upon being asked by our friends why he hadn't tipped them off at the time Rockwell started his drive from the vineyard, Corning told them that no horses had been missing then.

"That proves conclusively," he continued, "that we have a widespread organization to deal with, in fact, I've heard that their operations extend clear down to Pennsylvania, and I believe it.

"Furthermore, I think that we ought to call in the State authorities to cope with the situation. I have but little faith in your Sheriff Van Auken here."

"Neither have I," murmured Uncle Wilson.

Corning stayed with our friends that day; they took a trip to the cave exploring it thoroughly.

"Well," said Corning before they parted, "I wonder what new hiding place they'll find next; it looks to me as if you fellers had about all their guns spiked by now.

CHAPTER XXIII

THE END OF THE LOOMIS GANG

ONE week after the incident at the cave, Rockwell was taking leave from the Loomis boys after a most successful delivery of horses to them. They had enjoyed a good laugh when he told the boys how neatly he had trapped his neighbor, Josh, at the cave.

Said "Wash": "Bill you are learning fast. You are a worthy member and a credit to our gang."

His parting from Cornelia was even harder than on the previous occasion. She was ready to ride with him again, but "Big Bill" rode back in his carriage. This time "Big Bill" traveled with his men on their return trip, homeward bound. "Wash" accompanied his friend for a few miles before they finally parted, after a hearty handshake.

Had they but known that this was to be their last farewell and that "Wash" would meet his fate in the then near future. It is indeed a blessing that the future is a closed book to us all.

"Wash" was killed by the enraged farmers, as we have stated in a previous chapter. His brothers carried on their nefarious operations for several years longer, until their stronghold was burned down by a posse and the family was scattered to the four winds. Just prior to that, some indictments had been found against the remaining brothers. Those indictments were kept in the court house at Morrisville, which was then the county seat.

Suddenly and mysteriously the court house burned down. It was found out after a thorough investigation that the fire had been of incendiary origin and the finger of suspicion pointed heavily toward the Loomis brothers.

That was the last straw. Their punishment was dealt out summarily shortly after. The long suffering farmers had avenged themselves.

107

CHAPTER XXIV

A Holdup

"BIG BILL" also, had nearly reached the end of his rope, as Josh had predicted. Tempestuous times awaited him on his home-coming.

He stayed with his men until they neared the city of Auburn, when he instructed them to drive on home without him, as he had to even up a score with a certain party in that city.

Arrived in Auburn, he drove directly to the Osborn house, one of the leading hotels at that time. It was patronized by the sporting fraternity of the town.

Evidently "Big Bill" was well and favorably known there, because the proprietor greeted him cordially, asking him how long he intended to stay.

"That all depends on what luck I'll have. The bunch cleaned me out the last time I was here," answered Rockwell.

"You better go up then, there is a game on now."

There was a game in progress in a room on the second floor. As "Big Bill" walked over to the table, where they were playing, someone asked him to sit in.

"No, boys, I'm not going to stay," he said. He watched the game for awhile, apparently with little interest, cool and calculating. There happened to be a good sized stake on the table at one time.

"Big Bill" whipped a gun out of his pocket and pointing it in the general direction of the astonished players, he said in a deadly, quiet voice: "Don't move, boys, you know me; I'm Bill Rockwell."

Taken completely by surprise, the players never made a move, as he reached across the table, scooped up the money and put it in a bag he carried with him. Not a word was spoken.

"Big Bill" then backed out of the room, rushed downstairs, got his horse and was gone before the gamblers recovered from their shock.

Strange as it may appear, no one followed him and "Big Bill" drove off unmolested. Such was his reputation as a desperado, that he was given a wide berth wherever he went. They all had a wholesome respect for his marksmanship, which had been proven on many occasions.

When Rockwell reached home, he threw the bag of money on the table, telling his wife to buy a new dress for herself. Upon opening the bag and counting the money, she found seven hundred dollars.

Rockwell was the proud possessor of a costly rifle, which he guarded jealously. He used to put up a target on the west shore of Owasco Lake, the lake being about a mile wide at this point.

Sometimes he would invite his neighbors for target practice. They would shoot at the target from the east shore of the lake where "Big Bill's" boathouse was located. Try as they might, they could not compete with him; he would surpass them all.

He was the best marksman in the Finger Lakes region, if not in the state. His townsmen all feared him. There was something about the man they could not fathom, some hidden power; he impressed them as almost uncanny.

Although they mistrusted and disliked him for his shiftless habits, they could not help but admire him for his prowess with the rifle. "Big Bill" always carried his rifle with him on his peddling trips. Invariably he would visit the county fairs in the surrounding counties, where he was wont to sell his medicine.

In order to draw a crowd he used to stand up a manikin, carried with him for that purpose, place a clay pipe in the mouth of the same, stand off two hundred paces and shatter the pipe to fragments with a ball from his rifle. He had a standing offer of ten dollars to anyone who could duplicate his feat.

A humorous incident took place at a county fair in Cortland in connection with his shooting exhibition. "Big Bill" had his manikin propped up outside the fair grounds, and a large crowd had assembled to watch his shooting. The pipe was in place, "Big Bill" stepped back and took careful aim. One of the by-standers, more curious than the others, stood rather close to the target. Such confidence in "Big Bill's" accurate shooting did his spectators have, that they ventured nearer than prudence would warrant. This one man in particular stood within a few feet of the manikin, calmly puffing away at his pipe. "Big Bill's" rifle swerved just a trifle, and bang went the unsuspecting farmer's pipe to smithereens. He dropped as if he were shot instead of his pipe.

Everyone around there thought that the man was hit, and they stood petrified. "Big Bill" ran over to where the scared farmer lay and helped him to his feet. Laughing loudly, he slapped him on the back, handed him a ten dollar bill and said: "Go and buy yourself another pipe; the temptation was too great; I simply couldn't help myself."

"Big Bill's" Rifle

"Big Bill's" mirth was infectuous; a roar went up from the crowd and they all cheered him for his unexcelled marksmanship. The farmer who had so unwittingly furnished a target for "Big Bill," still dazed, felt himself all over. Finding himself unharmed, he started to walk away amid the jeers and gibes of his fellows.

"Big Bill" called him back and still laughing, he addressed him with these words: "You're just the man I want, I'll make you a good offer. If you travel with me, I'll give you ten dollars for every time you'll let me shoot a pipe out of your mouth."

"You go to h-ll," said the farmer, and went into the fair grounds.

"Big Bill" then produced his wares which, as usual, found a ready market because he had the crowd with him. After all he was a likable rogue.

CHAPTER XXV

A Close Call

TIMBERING or logging was one of the principal industries of this region, at that particular time. Martin Smith, owner of the Cascade Hotel, on the extreme southern end of Owasco Lake, was heavily interested in logging operations. The Cascade house with its miniature waterfalls, known as the Cascades, whence the hotel derives its name, later came into possession of the Hewett family.

The Cascade House was built in a wonderful location, commanding a fine view of the lake. The hotel enjoyed a large patronage, not only from the inhabitants of the Finger Lakes region, but from people from all over the state. It is visited by tourists from all over the country at the present day.

Martin Smith used to buy up logs and ship them to Prison City at the further, or northern end of the lake. There were other shippers, but Smith practically controlled the output at Owasco Lake.

The logs would be formed into rafts, held together by chains, after they had reached the lake. Big spikes were fastened to the links of the chains, a certain distance apart, the spikes to be driven into the logs, binding them together. The chains, known as rafting chains, were jealously guarded, because they were very expensive and hard to procure. Occasionally, a set of rafting chains would be lost in the lake and sometimes they would be stolen.

Luke Sackett, a small operator in the logging business, missed a set of his chains one day. He suspected Lige Shaw, an erratic colored man, who lived in his neighborhood, of having taken them.

Lige lived all alone in an old, tumble-down, two-story frame house. Lige used to play the violin at parties and family gather-

113

ings and he would do odd jobs for his neighbors. He was well
known all through the Finger Lakes region. Everybody considered him as harmless as a kitten and he was quite a local
character.

Sackett went to Lige's house, accusing him of stealing his
chains. Naturally, Lige denied the theft, disclaiming all
knowledge of the whereabouts of Luke's rafting chains.

Southern Shore of Owasco Lake

Unconvinced, Luke entered the house and searched the first
floor. Lige voiced no objection and offered no resistance.
Finding no sign of his chains, he started to go upstairs to look
over the second floor. Lige, who had been watching him closely,
shouted a warning, telling Luke at the same time: "You won't
find them chains up there either, but if you're bound to go up,
you'll smell hell and brimstone."

Paying no attention to Lige, whom no one ever took seriously,
Luke ascended the stairs. He ransacked the second floor and

was about to relinquish his search, when he discovered his rafting chains under a pile of old carpets in one of the bed rooms.

Picking up his chains, he started to leave, when to his horror, he saw the stairway in flames and found his retreat cut off. Lige had made good his bluff. His only way of escape lay through one of the windows.

Time was short, he had to act quickly. He fastened one end of his chain to the leg of a bedstead, dropping the other end through a window. Climbing out through the window, he let himself down hand over hand until he reached terra firma in safety. He looked around for Lige, but the old darky was missing. The house burned down to the ground.

CHAPTER XXVI

JOSHUA'S ARREST

MARTIN SMITH, proprietor of the Cascade House, next reported the loss of a set of rafting chains. He had learned from Luke Sackett what had happened to his chains and where and how he had recovered them.

Smith set out to locate Lige Shaw, the colored man, taking it for granted that Lige was implicated in the theft of his chains also, but Lige was nowhere to be found. He had taken French leave.

While Smith was on Lige's trail, he happened to meet Brow Scott, who volunteered his services in recovering Smith's missing chains.

Mindful of the old saying, "It takes a thief to catch a thief," Smith accepted the offer and promised Scott fifty dollars if he would succeed in locating his stolen property. He also notified the sheriff and offered a reward of fifty dollars for the return of his chains and no questions asked.

One evening, some two weeks later, as Josh, his father and his sister Ellen, were enjoying a quiet evening at home, they heard someone driving into the yard. Josh went out, to find Sheriff Van Auken, his brother-in-law, Brow Scott, and Martin Smith of the Cascade House, coming toward the house.

Josh was wondering what their presence at that late hour could mean. After an exchange of greetings, the sheriff stepped forward, informing Josh that he was under suspicion of having stolen Martin Smith's rafting chains and that they had come to look for them. Josh was thunderstruck. He could hardly find words to protest his innocence.

When old John, who had made his appearance in the meantime, recognized Brow Scott, his worthless son-in-law, he immediately started for him, cursing him. The sheriff restrained

117

him, assuring Josh that he considered him innocent, but inasmuch as Smith had taken out a search warrant for his place, it was his duty to serve it.

Smith and the sheriff then started for the barn to look for the chains, Josh and his father close at their heels.

Ellen came running out of the house just then and catching hold of her father, she implored him not to let them take her

Cascade House

children away. The poor, harassed woman was under the impression that Brow Scott, her shiftless husband, had invoked the law to gain possession of their two children, as he had threatened to do before. Her father calmed her down, telling her it was Josh they were after and not her children, advising her to go back in the house. Instead of doing so, Ellen left the yard and started on a run in the direction of Uncle Wilson's place.

Brow Scott was walking aimlessly around in the barnyard. He seemed ill at ease. As soon as Smith and the sheriff came out of the barn, Scott walked over to a strawstack, built up in the yard, and fumbled around in there. The others were watching him curiously. They were dumbfounded, to put it mildly, when Scott pulled some chains out from under the stack and started to drag them slowly in the sheriff's direction.

"You dirty dog," cried out Josh, who was the first to break the silence, and he made a leap for Scott.

The sheriff stepped between them. Smith then came forward, and examining the chains closely, he claimed them as his own.

Telling Josh he had better submit quietly, the sheriff then snapped handcuffs on him. Josh offered no resistance.

Unexpectedly, Uncle Wilson, who had been summoned by Ellen, arrived on the scene. Ellen, who was all out of breath, came close behind him.

"What's going on here?" asked Uncle Wilson quietly, as he surveyed the scene before him grimly.

On perceiving the handcuffs on Josh's wrists, Uncle Wilson moved over to the sheriff's side, grabbed him by the shoulder with one huge paw and holding him in a grip of iron, he thundered: "Take them off and be d——n quick about it, before I break your shoulder, you miserable blunderer. What right have you to put handcuffs on an innocent man? Don't you know that in this country of ours a man is innocent until he's proven guilty. This man is no criminal, but there are some criminals not very far from here, that you should adorn with iron bracelets, but you dare not, you coward."

The sheriff winced under Uncle Wilson's powerful grip, it was hard telling which hurt him the most, the physical pain or the tongue lashing he received. He begged to be released. He then made haste to remove the handcuffs from Josh's wrists.

"This boy is going to stay right here," declared Uncle Wilson. "We'll all be down to the village in the morning. In the meantime, I'll go security for him. You can hold me responsible. I guess my word is as good as that dirty skunk's over there," indicating Brow Scott, who slunk away in the darkness.

The sheriff then left with Smith, who had been a silent spectator to this remarkable proceeding.

There was very little sleep for Josh that night, or for his father and Uncle Wilson either. It was like a bolt out of a clear sky. Our three friends sat up most all night, too excited to sleep, discussing the matter from all angles.

That's Rockwell's doing. If there is any judgment in the land, he will get his punishment for it, was their unanimous opinion. "Yes, but Brow Scott planted the chains where he found them," commented Josh.

Uncle Wilson's Home

On the following morning our three friends went to the village. Accompanied by the sheriff they drove to the home of a justice of the peace where they had a preliminary hearing. Smith had sworn out a warrant for the arrest of Josh, who was released on a bail bond of two hundred dollars, signed by Uncle Wilson. His case was to go before the grand jury which would be in session in Auburn a month later.

Upon the sworn statements of Smith and Scott, Josh was indicted and a date was set for the trial. The impending trial created quite a commotion in that peaceful community.

Everybody talked about it and public sentiment was over-whelmingly in favor of Josh Rosecamp. Feeling ran high. On the day set for the trial, all those who could possibly leave home, flocked to the Court House at Auburn.

CHAPTER XXVII

A COURTROOM SCENE

THE courtroom was crowded when the case was called. Josh, his father and Uncle Wilson had arrived early and stood in earnest conversation. Ellen and Lu were also present. Smith and Scott were conversing with the district attorney, when Rockwell, with Cale Parmer at his side, joined their group.

The case was called. Martin Smith was the first witness for the prosecution. He was duly sworn, and upon being questioned by the district attorney, he stated when his rafting chains were stolen and where and how they were found.

Brow Scott followed him on the witness stand and told how the chains had been discovered by him under a strawstack on the Rosecamp farm.

Cale Parmer was next called by the prosecution. Everybody wondered what interest Cale could possibly have in the case, his name not having been mentioned in connection with it before. The people were not to be left in doubt for long and a surprise was in store for them.

After the usual questions the district attorney asked Parmer where he had been on the night Smith's chains were stolen. He allowed Parmer to tell the story in his own way, which he did as follows: "Scott and I went down to the village that night. We stayed there till about eleven o'clock when we started to walk home. We were about halfway home when we heard a rig coming up behind us. As the team and wagon came closer, we hid in the bushes alongside of the road, to see if the driver was someone we knew. If so, we were going to ask him for a ride.

"It turned out to be Josh Rosecamp with his team, and as we were not on good terms with him, we let him pass. As he drove past our hiding place, we heard a peculiar clanking sound come

123

from his wagon box. We made up our minds to find out what caused the funny noise.

"It was a dark night and the clanking sound combined with the rattling noise of the wagon, made it possible for us to sneak up behind the wagon, without being seen or heard by Josh. We examined his load, finding a set of rafting chains, covered up with some bags."

There was a tense moment in that courtroom. The silence was oppressive, as Parmer left the witness stand and Scott was recalled. Scott corroborated all that Parmer had stated. After a few minor questions, the district attorney turned suddenly upon Scott and demanded in an angry voice: "Why didn't you tell us about that when you were on the witness stand before?"

"You didn't ask me," was Scott's flippant answer.

Rockwell was the next and last witness called by the state. All eyes were focused on him as he sat in the witness chair, as unconcerned as could be. He possessed a wonderful self-control, and with a smile he turned to the prosecutor, who began to question him.

District attorney: "Do you know this defendant?"

Witness: "Yes, he is my neighbor."

District attorney: "Did you ever have any conversation with him, regarding Martin Smith's lost chains?"

Witness: "Yes."

District attorney: "State when and where."

Witness: "A few days after I heard the chains were stolen. In the road, in front of my place."

District attorney: "What did you say to the defendant on that occasion?"

Witness: "I asked him if he knew anything about Smith's rafting chains."

District attorney: "What did the defendant say? Give his exact words."

Witness: "He said, 'that's none of your d———d business, but I know where they are. What are you going to do about it?' "

District attorney: "Is that all?"

Witness: "That's all."

An ominous murmur could be heard among the spectators and the judge had to rap for order.

Josh next occupied the chair. He testified in his own behalf. He had engaged no lawyer. He knew he was innocent and hoped to prove it to the satisfaction of the twelve jurors. He felt confident that truth must prevail in the end.

He presented rather a weak alibi when he stated that he had been to Uncle Wilson's until ten o'clock on the night Smith's chains were stolen. From there he had gone home and retired. It was quite a contrast between Josh, who told his story in an open, straightforward manner, protesting his innocence, and his unprincipled accusers who sat uneasy, shooting furtive glances around the courtroom.

The case looked rather unfavorable for Josh, when Dr. Cooper, who was among the audience, and who had been an attentive listener to the proceedings, edged his way to the front. Addressing the judge, he politely asked permission to say a few words, as he had important information to bring before the court, in connection with this case.

The judge assented, despite the fact that it was rather an unusual request and irregular in the extreme. The eminent doctor took the stand. The tension in the courtroom was released. A ray of hope appeared as the well known Dr. Cooper, loved and respected by rich and poor alike, started to speak.

Dr. Cooper was not only a physician but a man as well. Everyone in that courtroom instinctively knew that Josh had found a new champion.

Dr. Cooper stated that on a certain day, some time after Smith's chains had been stolen, one Lige Shaw came to him for treatment. That upon investigation, he found the patient in a highly nervous condition, bordering on hysteria. His suffering seemed to be more mental than physical and he was all unstrung.

"I asked Lige what the trouble was," continued the good doctor, "and told him that unless he relieved his mind and made a clean breast of it, there would be no help for him. Easily intimidated, as most all colored people are, Lige then confessed to me.

"He told me that he had stolen Martin Smith's rafting chains at the instigation of William Rockwell, who gave him a ten dollar bill to do the job. That he was to receive ten dollars more if he delivered the chains to Brow Scott, which he did."

At last it was out. The mystery was solved. A shout of rage went up from the large assemblage as the venerable doctor delivered this damning bit of evidence and a scene, such as has never been equalled in any courtroom, before or since, followed. Pandemonium reigned.

The twelve jurors, to a man, leaped over the railing, which divided the jury box from the rest of the court room and made for Rockwell. "Big Bill" gave one look and started for the door, which he reached in safety. Out through the door and into the street he sped, closely followed by the twelve jurors and a surging, pushing mob behind. "Big Bill's" wonderful physique stood him in good stead, enabling him to keep the lead. He easily outdistanced his pursuers. Pell mell, through the streets of Auburn passed the strange race of pursuers and pursued.

Right up to the city line did the twelve men, good and true, continue the chase, before they stopped. Rockwell kept on going and he was never seen in these parts thereafter.

He procured a horse, hastened to his house, picked up some of his personal belongings, hitched up the fastest horse in the stable, and to express it in our vernacular, he beat it.

To his startled wife he told a different story from the true one. He made her believe, at least he thought he did, that he became involved in a fight at the village and that he was compelled to

leave town for a few weeks.   Nothing new for the poor woman.
She was used to his prolonged periods of absence by that time.
Before he left he told his wife that Cale Parmer and Brow
Scott would look after her while he was gone.

CHAPTER XXVIII

ROCKWELL'S EXIT

CALE PARMER had been arrested with Henry Bates and Charles Tidd as an accessory after the fact in the theft of Milo Cox's horses. He was out on bail when he testified in the trial of Martin Smith vs. Joshua Rosecamp. He was tried later on, found guilty and sentenced to a term in Auburn state prison. After serving some time, part of his sentence was remitted, with the understanding that he leave the county, which he did. He followed his chieftain into exile, joining "Big Bill" in Owego, whither he had fled.

This was merely another instance where one of Rockwell's lieutenants, after faithfully carrying out his instructions, had landed in prison, rather than to incriminate "Big Bill," who had planned the theft of Milo Cox's horses.

Parmer was met and recognized by a former acquaintance from Moravia, after he had been in Owego for a short time. Shaking hands with him, the man addressed him by his name. Stubbornly denying his identity, Cale said: "You got me wrong, my friend, my name ain't Cale Parmer." Cale went out West and was killed.

Thus Cale Parmer passes out of the story.

Brow Scott, who kept in touch with "Big Bill" after his sudden exit from Moravia, assisted Mrs. Rockwell in packing her household goods, helping her and her three boys move to Owego, where she was met by her husband.

A warrant was issued for Scott's arrest for his part in the theft of Martin Smith's rafting chains. It was never served, the people of Moravia considering themselves fortunate to be rid of him.

And so passes Brow Scott.

129

A sigh of relief went up and many a silent prayer was offered by the old settlers of Moravia and surroundings, when Rockwell and his lawless gang had been driven out of town and county.

Great rejoicing was heard on all sides, when the "Terror of the Finger Lakes region" was finally banished.

The Loomis brothers carried on operations long after Rockwell had been driven out of Cayuga County, and even after "Wash," the oldest brother had been killed.

Just prior to the burning of the Court House at Morrisville, and while "Wash" was still alive, Bill Abell, a farmer who lived at the head of the Cherry Valley turnpike, lost a black mare which had been running loose in his pasture.

Grove, the second oldest of the Loomis boys, had been seen driving the mare. Their place was searched as before, without any result. Grove was duly arrested and lodged in jail.

Abell called on a certain man who stood close to the Loomis boys, and asked him if he could assist him in recovering his mare, promising that he would drop proceedings against Grove, providing he got his horse back.

This man went to see "Wash" Loomis and laid the proposition before him. "Leave it to me," said "Wash," "I'll see that Bill Abell gets his horse back." A week later the black mare was back in Abell's pasture. The horse had been shipped to a certain town in Pennsylvania and "Wash" had sent his brother Denio, called the "judge," after it.

While Grove was confined in jail, his brother "Wash" came to see him.   After the two brothers had conversed for awhile, "Wash" mentioned in a casual way that Grove wore a pair of heavy cowhide boots. So he said to Grove: "Say, you ain't got any use for them boots while you are in here, suppose that we trade. you can wear my shoes. I could use your boots to better advantage on the farm."

Grove readily consented, so they traded footwear right then and there. No one being present to watch them while the swap was made, "Wash" reached his hand into the boots, which Grove had kicked off, and extracted therefrom a nice wad of counterfeit money, transferring it to his trousers pocket. This only goes to prove that lawyer Spriggs was correct in recognizing "Wash's" ability and cleverness when he made the statement: "We can try a case, but no one can plan it like 'Wash' can."

One time "Wash" was arrested for having a horse in his possession that had been stolen in Oswego County. He was taken to Oswego to be tried. The judge who presided at the trial, was a good lawyer and a brilliant orator. He had the habit, or call it misfortune, to contort his features while talking. So, while the judge was addressing the jury, everybody naturally watched his face. "Wash" wasn't very slow to notice this, and while everybody's attention was riveted on the judge, "Wash" quietly stole out of the courtroom and was gone before they missed him. He reached home in safety and immediately sent the stolen horse back to its owner by one of his brothers. Consequently the case against him was dropped.

"Big Bill" made at least one more delivery of horses to the Loomis boys after he was banished from Cayuga County. Brow Scott and Cale Parmer both were with him on this occasion. Whether he found it too hazardous or found the distance too great, we do not know, but according to our records this was his last trip to the Loomis brothers' place.

On this occasion "Big Bill" arrived unexpectedly. After he had dismounted he inquired for "Wash," and after being told by Grove, the second oldest of the Loomis boys, that "Wash" had been killed by a posse of farmers a short time before, he became furious. He and "Wash" had been the closest of friends, and they had so much in common that they were like two brothers.

The Loomis girls were all at home. Cornelia was overjoyed at seeing Rockwell again. Absence makes the heart grow fonder. Her spirits fell when "Big Bill" informed her that in all probability this would be their last meeting. It turned out to be.

The poor unsophisticated girl—better for her peace of mind

had they never met. Yet, 'tis said—better to have loved in vain, than not to have loved at all.

"Big Bill" confided to Grove what had happened to him in Auburn, and that he was practically an exile. He admitted shamefacedly how Josh Rosecamp had bested him after all.

"Never you mind, Bill, you can stay with us," said Grove consolingly, "'Wash', our leader, is dead, and I don't know of any one who is better qualified to take his place than you. You're a great traveler, known all over; you can do the buying and we will attend to the shipping as before."

Grove continued: "The farm next to ours is for sale; it can be bought cheap. You could move here with your family, and we would form a combination that's hard to beat."

Cornelia, who had been listening to their conversation, now spoke up and entreated "Big Bill" to act on her brother's advice. But "Big Bill" was adamant in turning their offer down.

"You see, it's like this", he added, "it got too warm for me in Richport, so I moved to Moravia, from where they drove me out. If I located here, they would soon get wise to me. Just now, I'm stopping at Owego. How long I'll remain there I don't know, but I've got to lay low for awhile. My intention is to go further west where I'm not known, but I've a mission to fulfill, before I leave here," concluded "Big Bill."

"Big Bill" appeared very anxious to learn the names of the different members of the posse that killed his friend "Wash." He tried to persuade Grove to accompany him and point out to him where they lived. Grove asked him what he intended to do, but "Big Bill" refused to enlighten him on the subject.

At all events Grove considered it unwise to make the rounds of the farmers in their vicinity, and as he said, it would be like issuing a challenge to them. "Why, it would be like disturbing a hornet's nest. Lord knows, we are disliked enough now," concluded Grove with a wry smile on his face.

But Grove had reckoned without his sister, for Cornelia spoke up then, and volunteered her services to go with Rockwell wherever and whenever he chose. Cornelia had seen the members of the posse on that fateful night when her brother "Wash" had been killed and her brother Grove mortally wounded. With a woman's keen observation she had recognized them all, for they wore no masks.

Consequently, on the following morning, Cornelia and "Big Bill" started out on horseback,—to show him the country, as she smilingly asserted.

Evidently, Joshua's horse wasn't used to a strange rider yet. After Cornelia had mounted, the horse bucked and reared, and tried in every way to shake the girl off. At times the horse would stand almost straight up on its hind legs, but it was no use, Cornelia proved its master. She rode astride, and used neither whip nor spur.

"Big Bill" was delighted, and he admired her horsemanship. All the Loomis girls could ride, but Cornelia surpassed them all.

They rode all that forenoon, Cornelia pointing out the house of every farmer that had been a member of that memorable posse. To say that Cornelia enjoyed the ride, is putting it mildly; the poor girl had never been so happy before. Gladly would she have laid down her life for her companion, had he so desired. "Big Bill" was the first real man, according to her conception, that had come into her life, and she was completely infatuated.

They returned home from their ride about noon. After dinner "Big Bill" declared his intention to start on his journey for home that night, saying: "You know, my friends, I'm a good ways from home now and I've got a long ride ahead of me."

Accordingly, "Big Bill" and his men, Brow Scott and Cale Parmer, set out that night on their homeward journey. After a tearful parting and a fond embrace from the fair Cornelia (he had to promise her to come back), "Big Bill" shook hands all around, swung himself in the saddle and was gone, followed by his two satellites. That was the last ever seen of "Big Bill" in that section of the country.

On that same night numerous farmers' barns in that locality burned down. By a queer coincidence, every farmer whose barn had been destroyed, had been a member of the posse who was responsible for "Wash" Loomis' death.

It was the worst conflagration that ever happened in those parts, and there are some old settlers still living, who remember it to this day.

After an uneventful trip, Rockwell and his men returned to Owego. He lived there for three years.

Horses disappeared mysteriously in that locality as had been the case when "Big Bill" lived first in Richport, later in Moravia. Rumors floated around thick and fast connecting "Big Bill" with their disappearance.

His outlet for stolen horses was then in Pennsylvania where he had made new friends and found other confederates.

Following a stay of three years, Rockwell moved to some town in Ohio, where he built a pretentious home for his family. Evidently he had done well at his trade. Be that as it may, he left a considerable fortune at the time of his death.

Rockwell's farm was placed in the hands of a land agent, to come later on, by the strange irony of fate, in the possession of a member of the Rosecamp family. Horace Rosecamp owns it to-day.

Lige Shaw, the colored man, who had confessed to Dr. Cooper, admitting that he stole Smith's rafting chains, thereby exonerating Josh, tried to pass the ten dollar bill given him by Brow Scott for his services. It turned out to be a counterfeit. Hard luck!

Poor Lu died on the eve of her marriage to Josh. Josh was heartbroken. They had looked forward to a happy married life after all their trials and tribulations. The ways of a Divine Providence are sometimes hard to fathom and still harder to understand.

Josh sold the old homestead after his father's death and bought a small farm east of Moravia, close to the village. He continued raising horses with the able assistance of Jack Feek.

Josh became known as the most successful breeder and trainer of fast horses in that part of the state. In due time he was married to Cordelia Moore, whose father owned the adjoining farm.

Ellen, sister of Josh, married a respectable farmer. She was compensated for the failure of her first marital venture. Her former married life seemed like a bad dream to her.

Uncle Wilson, who lived to a ripe old age, often came to visit Josh in his new home. They would spend many hours together, talking about their strange adventures and recalling the stirring incidents of former days.

In later years, Josh would spend hours telling his son Melvin the history of his younger days, supplemented by his diary. His remarkable experiences were always uppermost in his mind and it was his greatest desire to see the story in print. His wish was not to be gratified. His son Melvin, in accordance with his father's wishes and by his untiring efforts, finally succeeded in having the story published.

CHAPTER XXIX

CONCLUSION

THE quaint old village of Moravia hasn't changed much during all these years, and the Moravia House, which figures prominently in this story, is today known as the principal hotel there. Moravia, originally called Owasco Flats, still flourishes and it is at present one of the prettiest villages in the State.

It was settled by the Holland Land Co. in the early part of the seventeenth century. The greater part of the inhabitants of Moravia and surrounding towns are descendants of those early Holland-Dutch settlers.

They came of sturdy stock and they were instrumental in transforming a wilderness into one of the best and most productive farming sections of the Empire State. The hamlet of Owasco, meaning "Long Bridge," according to Indian lore, was also developed by the Holland-Dutch pioneers.

The Cascade House, at the head of Owasco Lake, too, survives and is still doing a flourishing business. Tourists from every part of our country are visiting there every year to enjoy the beautiful scenery surrounding it, and to go boating and fishing on beautiful Owasco Lake.

The cave, where Joshua was imprisoned, is still in existence, so is the vineyard and also Hewett's gully—mute evidence of the strange happenings of former days.

The old Rosecamp homestead has been abandoned ever since old John died and it lies in ruins. The old Rockwell farmhouse, headquarters of "Big Bill," where many a dark plot was hatched out, burned down a few years ago and is also in ruins.

Cale Parmer's home, the "house of mystery," still stands. The house and farm is owned by a Rosecamp today, who works it better than Cale Parmer ever did. It is one of the finest farms on that hillside.

The road leading past the old Rockwell home, to the village of Moravia, has been christened "Rockwell drive." At whose instigation, or who the sponsor was, the author is unable to tell, unless it was a descendant of Rockwell, hoping to remove the stigma attached to his name. Certainly "Big Bill" had no desire to have his name perpetuated in a community which drove him out of their midst.

Logging operations have long since ceased. The woods have been cleared off, fertile fields have taken their place.

Horsebreeding has been relegated to the rear, except for farm use. Automobiles have replaced horse-drawn vehicles, as elsewhere.

Wonderful scenery meets the eye on all sides. The Finger Lakes region is the show place of our country. Its beauty is unexcelled. It is almost inconceivable to link this wonderful spot of mother earth with the dark and sinister deeds committed on its face in the days gone by. To think that this quiet and peaceful countryside formed a stage for "Big Bill" to act upon and present his daring show! From the mouths of the oldest inhabitants one can still hear the strange stories of "'Big Bill' Rockwell, who was too wise to be caught" and of "Joshua, the man of the Finger Lakes region."

This is book Number One, and will soon be followed by book Number Two, which will deal with the descendants of the characters in this book. It will also give a description of the Finger Lakes region as it appears today.

Negotiations are pending for the filming of this gripping story and its early appearance on the silver screen is assured.

There may be a doubt in the minds of some of our readers about this story being based on truth, and it is not to be wondered at. However, we have statements from reputable people, affirming the facts in the case. We are also in possession of indictments against Wm. Rockwell and his accomplices for various crimes.   Those indictments were procured at the courthouse in the city of Auburn.

Thus ends one of the most remarkable stories ever written— a story that rivals the most exciting tales of the wild West. Traveling through the picturesque Finger Lakes Region today, which is visited by thousands of tourists from all over our country yearly, it seems almost unbelievable that the scenes depicted in this book were ever enacted there.   Truth is stranger than fiction indeed!

Future editions will chronicle additional historical events of the early life in the Finger Lakes Region.

(THE END)

APPENDIX

IN order to enlighten our readers as to the true personality of "Big Bill" Rockwell, or rather those readers who have not already guessed his identity, this appendix has been added to the book. It will be shown that Wm. Rockwell led a dual life, a veritable Dr. Jekyll and Mr. Hyde existence.

At home he was known as Wm. A. Rockefeller, while on his travels he called himself either Dr. Livingston or William May. Rockefeller was an adventurous character, who in the disposure of the employments of his brain thought fit to make fraud the master. He was a natural fakir with a mind inexhaustibly rich in all of the resources of imposture, and was acquainted with every artifice which makes falsehood look like truth and ignorance like knowledge.

Upon his trips away from home William A. Rockefeller went under an assumed name, often appearing under the name of Livingston.

At Burford, Canada, under this alias, he married in the 50s, Miss Margaret Allen, the daughter of a Canadian farmer. In Freeport, Illinois, Dr. Livingston was the same roving, mysterious person he had been in New York State. He would be gone for months and come back with a great roll of money which he would display. He would go to small towns and put up at a hotel for a week or so, getting out hand-bills advertising himself as "The Celebrated Dr. Livingston." He advertised to cure anything but made a specialty of cancers. He also traveled under the alias of William May.

For a period of fifty years "Dr." Rockefeller is known to have led this strange sort of double life, and for thirty-four of these years he had two wives, one Eliza Davison Rockefeller, the mother of the oil magnate; the other, Margaret Allen Livingston. The former he married in 1837, and she died in New York City in 1889, unaware of her husband's deception.

The latter he married in Ontario, Cánada, in 1855, and she is said to have been ignorant of his previous marriage until after his death.

During the latter part of his life he lived much of the time under the name of "Dr. William Livingston" but occasionally appeared at the homes of his sons and old acquaintances under the name of William Rockefeller. He had amassed a considerable fortune at the time of his death and there wasn't any doubt in the minds of those who knew him best, that this money laid the foundation for the Rockefeller millions.

—THE AUTHOR

www.ingramcontent.com/pod-product-compliance
Lightning Source LLC
LaVergne TN
LVHW091219080426
835509LV00009B/1075